PLANT BASED DIET

COOKBOOK FOR BEGINNERS

A kick-start Guide with lot of Delicious and Healthy Whole Food Recipes that will Make you Drool. Includes a 30-Day Vegan Meal Plan for People & Athletes

Legal & Disclaimer

The information contained in this book and its contents is not designed to replace or take the place of any form of medical or professional advice; and is not meant to replace the need for independent medical, financial, legal or other professional advice or services, as may be required. The content and information in this book have been provided for educational and entertainment purposes only.

The content and information contained in this book have been compiled from sources deemed reliable, and it is accurate to the best of the Author's knowledge, information, and belief. However, the author cannot guarantee its accuracy and validity and cannot be held liable for any errors and/or omissions. Further, changes are periodically made to this book as and when needed. Where appropriate and/or necessary, you must consult a professional (including but not limited to your doctor, attorney, financial advisor or such other professional advisor) before using any of the suggested remedies, techniques, or information in this book.

Upon using the contents and information contained in this book, you agree to hold harmless the Author from and against any damages, costs, and expenses, including any legal fees potentially resulting from the application of any of the information provided by this book. This disclaimer applies to any loss, damages or injury caused by the use and application, whether directly or indirectly, of any advice or information presented, whether for breach of contract, tort, negligence, personal injury, criminal intent, or under any other cause of action.

You agree to accept all risks of using the information presented inside this book.

You agree that by continuing to read this book, where appropriate and/or necessary, you shall consult a professional (including but not limited to your doctor, attorney, or financial advisor or such other advisor as needed) before using any of the suggested remedies, techniques, or information in this book.

TABLE OF CONTENTS

INTRODUCTION

For centuries and all around the globe, people have different ways of eating. They have what they call staple foods and most would be surprised to hear that other peoples staple food is meat while the rest will be amazed that other individuals actually team corn and honey the staple food. The purpose of this book is to introduce the types of meals that are derived from non-animals' products.

By definition, a plant-based meal can be said to be any type of edible food that is only derived from plants. Even though plant-based meal can mean a lot of different things to all the people, generally it settles close to the plant products and also animal products such as eggs and milk but not meat. Types of plant-based meals include but not limited to; fruits, vegetables, legumes, nuts, grains, soy products, seeds, among other plant-based products. At the point when meat and meat items, and other animal-derived nourishments, for example, fish, dairy items, and eggs, are not eaten, the supplements which they contain should be gotten from different sources that are normally rich in those supplements or are braced. The general impact on the diet of barring these nourishments can prompt huge contrasts in the supplement admissions of veggie lovers and omnivores.

People have over time managed to interpret plant-based meals to other products that are inclusive of meat in the diet. That remains a controversy as different cultures have different beliefs. The rise of processed foods over the years has brought deceases and other challenges in the food industry. This is the reason why a good number of individuals have decided to turn to plant-based meals as they believe it reduces the chances of diseases and well as it being cost-effective in one way or another. People will argue that there is no difference in a full meal diet and a plant-based meal, but science has proven that they are indeed different.

Plant-based meals are considered to be healthier as compared to other types of meals. Fast food is the order of the day as the human race has become so busy to even take a look on their health meaning that it is possible for a large population to have grown far away from healthy living. This book emphasizes the importance of a healthy lifestyle as well as gives instructions on how to change and start on the journey of healthy living by incorporating a plant-based meal in each and everyone's meal plans. By choosing a healthy lifestyle, a person will be able to be in control of their body fat content and also check their weight as this will be more beneficial to them in a healthy way and guarantee them a life that is less of strange diseases with lots of expenses on drugs and checkups. It is no discussion that when one is leading a healthy lifestyle the most definitely are more energetic as compared to others.

CHAPTER 1:
WHY YOU SHOULD EAT VEGETABLES

Vegetables are basic for equilibrated abstains from food since they contribute a critical wellspring of nutraceuticals in day by day human life. The nutraceuticals are the substances found as a characteristic segment of nourishments or other ingestible structures that have been resolved to be gainful to the human body in counteracting or treating at least one maladies or in improving physiological execution past satisfactory healthful effects in a way that is important to either improved phase of wellbeing and prosperity and decrease of danger of illness.

There is a lot of enthusiasm for the scope of dietary practices pursued by veggie lovers, both regarding the wholesome substance of veggie lover diets, and wellbeing and mortality rates among veggie lovers. Notwithstanding the prevalent sentiment that vegetarianism is a sound alternative, there are a few territories for concern and cautious arranging is important to guarantee that the eating routine is very much adjusted. In parallel with this, there is a developing attention to the potential advantages of plant-based slims down, and even the individuals who incorporate meat in the eating routine are encouraged to eat more plant-inferred nourishments. There is an assortment of reasons why individuals are veggie lover or decide to maintain a strategic distance from a few or every single creature item, in spite of the fact that for most of individuals on the planet who do not eat meat, the explanations behind having a plant-based eating routine.

These segments can be valuable cell reinforcements, regular colorants (for example, carotenoids), minerals, nutrients, which regularly have included focal points. The advancement of solid vegetable items has matched with a flooding shopper intrigued by the sound usefulness of nourishment. Every vegetable involve a one of a kind blend of Phyto nutraceuticals which separate them from different vegetables. Vegetable admissions have been exceptionally associated with improved gastrointestinal wellbeing, diminished danger of coronary failure, a few kinds of disease, and ceaseless illnesses, for example, diabetes. This part makes an audit and examines the medical advantages of generally utilized vegetables.

Vegetables are a significant piece of smart dieting and are an important source of nutrition that is vital in our body. They include: calcium, vitamins, proteins, etc. some types of vegetables sweet potatoes, pumpkin, kales have some extra nutrients, thus very vital. Products of the soil are pieces of well, adjusted eating routine and can assist you with remaining solid. It's significant that you eat enough of them. Proof appears there are critical medical advantages to getting at any rate 5 parts of an assortment of products of the soil each day. That is 5 segments of leafy foods altogether, not 5 segments of each. Individuals who consume both vegetables and fruits every day usually have less chances of being affected by some common dangerous and deadly illnesses.

Keeping the body in good health and energetic is usually the function of the nutrition acquired when one takes vegetables. Vegetables contribute a significant wellspring of nutraceuticals for well-adjusted human eating routine. nutraceuticals are the substances found as a characteristic segment of nourishments or other ingestible structures that have been resolved to be helpful to the human body in anticipating or treating at least one sicknesses or in improving physiological execution past satisfactory dietary effects in a manner that is pertinent to either improved phase of wellbeing and prosperity and decrease of danger of illnesses. While the wholesome significance of vegetables has, for some time been perceived inside the nourishment and restorative networks, there is an expanding mindfulness among the overall population of the wellbeing points of interest of diets high in vegetables.

Numerous vegetable wares satisfy human caloric needs as a result of the sugars they contain, and vegetable harvest are particularly important wellspring of fundamental amino acids. Vegetables can play a much increasingly significant job in the nourishing nature of diets. This can be practiced through better scattering about their dietary benefit and through changes in dietary patterns that will profit individuals, particularly those on negligible eating regimens. By and by, vegetable generation in creating nations, shockingly, regularly plays an auxiliary job to unhealthy grain crops

The definite systems that can clearly explain how feeding on fruits and vegetables lead to a reduction in the chances of getting sick are not quite clearly known. However, some doctors and nutritionists suggest that elements found in the nutrients diminish the danger of constant infections, for example, malignant growth.

Vegetables give supplements, calories, nutrients and dietary filaments, which of parity back to eats less that take care of the nourishment that we need both an amount and quality issues. There is an expanding mindfulness among the overall population of the upsides of diets wealthy in vegetables that gives enough nutrients and micronutrients dietary strands, and phytochemicals that advance wellbeing. Along these lines there is a need to choose vegetables that are wealthy in phytochemicals and improved degree of nutraceuticals. The epidemiological proof to support expending diet that is high in products of the soil hushes up convincing. The proof of explicit vegetables and in fact explicit mixes is less persuading, albeit epidemiological investigations of malignancy propose that it is, for the most part, the exceptionally shaded green or yellow vegetables that are related with decreased frequency and death rates

Vegetables that are eaten every day have been proven to be in link with improvement of gastrointestinal wellbeing, coronary illness, diabetes, great wellbeing, stroke, iron deficiency, gastric ulcer among others. The most significant photo Nutriceuticals in vegetables that have natural action against interminable ailments are nutrients, minerals, dietary fiber, cancer prevention agents, carotenoids and flavonoids. Nutrients must be acquired from the eating routine, as the body can't create them in satisfactory sums. Citrus natural products, strawberries, green peppers, tomatoes, and kiwi are instances of nourishments high in nutrient C. All vegetables are wellsprings of nutrients and thusly have medical advantages Vitamins, for example, A, B6, C, and K are essential to the human body and can be given by vegetables. Vegetables have a lot of minerals which are required by the body for development and furthermore have certain medical advantages:

Dried beans, lentils, peas, just as the various vegetables and dull green verdant vegetables are particularly great wellsprings of iron, shockingly better on a for every calorie premise than meat.

Zinc is found in vegetables, for example, beans, peas, pumpkin seeds, ocean vegetables, and in nuts, almonds, entire grains, sunflower seeds, soy nourishments, and dark currant.

Some great wellsprings of dissolvable fiber are kidney beans, grain, wheat rich breakfast oats, and prepared potatoes with skin, spinach, oats, and popcorn. Nourishments wealthy in fiber fulfills hunger without contributing unnecessary calories in this manner helps weight reduction.

The primary Constituents of products of the soil that positively affect human wellbeing. The medical advantage of vegetables ought not be connected to just one compound or one kind of vegetable. However, a gathering of vegetable that give better security against certain constant expires.

Nutrient A - Essential for vision, skin, and the resistant framework. Advances development. Secures against certain kinds of malignancy. Melon, apricots, dull green, and profound yellow vegetables, for example, pumpkin, carrots, sweet potatoes, spinach, greens, and chime peppers.

Nutrient C - Strengthens veins, improves wound and bone recuperating, expands the protection from diseases, and builds the assimilation of iron – another significant supplement for development. Melon, honeydew melon, peaches, oranges, strawberries, kiwifruit, asparagus, sweet potatoes, chime peppers, broccoli.

Nutrient E - It is the significant lipid-dissolvable segment in the cell cancer for the prevention agent that works as the barrier. Oxidation is linked to a number of potential conditions and infectious diseases, including joint pain and waterfalls. Nuts (for example, almonds, cashew nuts, filberts, macadamias, walnuts, pistachios, and pecans).

Cancer prevention agents - Antioxidants are nutrients, minerals, and different substances that battle free radicals, which assume a job in the movement. Foods grown from the ground overflowing with shading, for example, berries, tomatoes, and malignant growths, coronary illness, eye infection, and others.

Cancer prevention agents shield the body from unfavorable organic responses, including oxygen. Cell reinforcements check or kill the hurtful impacts of free radicals. These go about as scroungers with the expectation of complimentary radicals and receptive oxygen species, in this manner keeping them from disturbing the concoction soundness of the cells.

Phytonutrients - of malignant growth and coronary illness. Phytonutrients are the shading colors in the leafy foods that either go about as cancer prevention agents or upgrade the cell reinforcement benefits. Dim green and profound yellow vegetable.

Fiber - Important to keep up stomach related wellbeing, just as decrease blood cholesterol. Raspberries, pears, blackberries, Brussels grows, parsnips, raisins, broccoli, dark beans. - Diabetes, coronary illness. Fiber content add to the medical advantage by improving gut travel, by overseeing blood glucose fixations, and by shipping through the human gut a noteworthy measure of Phyto nutraceuticals and minerals connected to the fiber framework.

The utilization of new vegetables gives the purchaser an assortment of aggravates that impact human wellbeing. The phytochemicals found in crisp vegetables have antiflammatory, chemical hindering, and bioactive highlights fit for fighting the exercises of oxidants.

Phytochemicals are natural mixes gotten from plants that have best wellbeing defensive impact just as ailment insurance and relapse. Other than the regular supplements, for example, starches, amino acids, and protein, there are sure non-supplement phytochemicals in vegetables that have natural movement against interminable sicknesses. They are low in fat and like all plant items, contain no cholesterol. Most phytochemicals are found in generally little amounts in vegetable yields.

Vegetables contain a huge number of gainful phytochemicals, notwithstanding the 14 nutrients and 16 minerals. A few phytochemicals are hearty cell reinforcements and are accepted to decrease the danger of some ceaseless infirmities. Vegetable consumption has been profoundly corresponded with improved gastrointestinal wellbeing and diminished danger of respiratory failure, a few kinds of malignancy, and ceaseless sicknesses, for example, diabetes. Henceforth, utilization of a vegetable-rich eating routine consistently has unquestionable constructive outcomes on wellbeing and is probably going to bear the cost of better insurance against a few incessant diseases.

The high utilization of tomatoes and tomato items has been connected to carcinogenesis decrease, particularly with respect to prostate malignant growth. Entire nourishments are progressively observed to be more advantageous to human wellbeing than detached parts, for example, supplements. Expanded utilization of carotenoid-rich vegetables beats carotenoid dietary supplements in expanding low-thickness lipoprotein oxidation obstruction, bringing down DNA harm. Potato is seen uniquely as a wellspring of starches, but on the other hand is an incredible wellspring of basic amino acids. It is said to give insurance against colon malignant growth, improves glucose resilience and insulin affectability, brings down plasma cholesterol and triglyceride focuses, expands satiety, and perhaps even decreases fat stockpiling. Eggplant is an amazing wellspring of assimilation steady with fiber and bone-building manganese, catalyzing catalyst molybdenum and potassium. The Eggplant is additionally a decent wellspring of bone-building nutrient K and magnesium just as copper, nutrient C, nutrient B6, folate, and niacin. Eggplant is also used for the treatment of high blood cholesterol and stabilization.

Cell reinforcement nutrients A and C help to anticipate cell harm, malignant growth, and illnesses identified with maturing, and they bolster insusceptible capacity. They additionally decrease aggravation like that found in joint pain and asthma. Nutrient K advances appropriate blood coagulating, fortifies bones, and shields cells from oxidative harm. With the regularly changing way of life of people, the cancer prevention agent safeguard frameworks are frequently over-burden bringing about oxidative pressure. Besides, the degrees of cell reinforcement guard instrument decline apparently with age. These may bring about the improvement of a considerable number of infections. Consequently, a normal utilization of vegetable-rich eating regimen has certain beneficial outcomes on wellbeing since Phyto nutraceuticals of vegetables can shield the human body from a few kinds of constant illnesses. The system by which vegetables decline danger of illness is intricate, and to a great extent, obscure however different parts of the entire nourishment are probably going to add to the general medical advantage. At long last it tends to be inferred that medical advantages can be improved by expanded utilization of vegetables as it contains immense phytochemicals, which might be a significant wellspring of dietary cancer prevention agents.

CHAPTER 2:
VEGETABLES ARE BETTER THAN MEAT

In many places on the planet, the utilization of meat is held in high regard and is broadly viewed as a nourishment item with high healthy benefit. Vegetable items has corresponded with a flooding buyer between tested in the sound usefulness of nourishment. Vegetables make up a significant bit of the eating regimen by keeping a close look at the very many things that people consume in the world and those that are known to assist nutrients such as dietary fiber, phytochemicals, and minerals also known as the phytonutriceuticals. Vegetable contains a novel blend of phytonutriceuticals; an extraordinary decent variety of vegetables ought to be eaten to guarantee that person's eating regimen incorporates a blend of phytonutriceuticals and to get all the medical advantages.

Vegetables are fundamental for well-adjusted eating regimens as they are responsible for the supply of nutrients, minerals, dietary fiber, and phytochemicals. Every vegetable gathering contains an extraordinary mix and measure of these phytonutriceuticals, which distinguishes them from different gatherings and vegetables within their own gathering. Vegetables are able to prevent cancer, and at the same time they are thought to minimize its dangers by detoxification of the agents that cause cancer.

Very good habits of eating vegetables has been proven to impact and lower cardiovascular problems in people. When one does not consume vegetables for a long time, the quality is not guaranteed.

For one to get the important nourishment, they have to look at quality and quantity of the vegetables that they consume in their everyday life and hence they have to know that important nutrients are available and supplements such as phytochemicals and dietary filaments are available which contain less calories but have a big percent in terms of nutrients.

There is an expanding mindfulness among the overall population of the upsides of diets rich in vegetables to guarantee admission of most vitamins and micronutrients, dietary filaments, and phytochemicals that advance wellbeing. The fundamental distinction is that each vegetable bunch contains a remarkable blend and measure phytonutriceuticals, which recognizes them from different gatherings and vegetables within their own gathering. Cruciferous vegetables which incorporate, cabbage, broccoli, cauliflower, Brussels grows, kales, turnip, rutabaga, radish, watercress, mustards, among different vegetables, give the most extravagant wellsprings of glucose- notates in the human eating regimen.

An eating routine wealthy in crucifers is probably going to secure people against colon and thyroid tumors, and when overcome with vegetables wealthy in different phytonutriceuticals, can ensure against malignancy in different organs. Every one of these crucifers additionally contains little measures of different glucosinolates. The greater part of the distinctions in the aliphatic glucosinolates is hereditarily managed. Crucifer vegetables are additionally plentiful in nutrients, with kale appraised as the second most elevated Crucifers likewise contain critical measures of dietary fiber.

Vegetarianism alludes to a big percentage of nutrients, as described by a researcher on plant nourishments and shirking of creature nourishments. vegetarians expend bird products, lactovegetarian's diet comprises of vegetables, grains, organic products, vegetables/nuts, as well as products that come from cows while semi-vegetarians confine to the exact opposite of active vegetarians as they consume fish, poultry products and meat. They can choose one of them or stick to all.

The term 'vegetarianism' alludes to a big spectrum of dietary examples described by an emphasizer on plant nourishments and shirking of creature food sources. Ovo-vegetarians devour lactovegetarian's, and eggs diet comprises of vegetables, grains, natural products, nuts, and vegetables, together with dairy items, while semi-vegetarians limit the kind of meat to as it were fish poultry or on the other hand both fish and poultry (pesco-pollo vegetarians). The term 'vegetarianism' alludes to a wide spectrum of dietary examples described by a researcher on plant nourishments and evasion of creature nourishments. Ovo-vegetarians devour eggs, lactovegetarian's diet comprises of vegetables, grains, natural products, nuts, and vegetables, together with milk and dairy items, while semi-vegetarians confine the kind of meat to as it were fish (pescovegetarian), poultry (poll vegetarian), or on the other hand both fish and poultry (pesco-pollovegetarians).

A vegan diet has been connected Trusted Source to a lower danger of cardiovascular hazards. It's been discovered that the more meat individuals expend, the higher their danger of type 2 diabetes. Veggie lover nourishment will, in general, be lower in fat, particularly immersed higher in fiber and fats, than creature-based food sources. A veggie lover doesn't eat meat or fish. However, there are various kinds of vegan. Some expend eggs and dairy items, while vegetarians, and eat no creature produce by any means, including nectar. A few people call themselves veggie lovers, yet they normally eat fish. It is not a must for a person to consume meat for them to acquire all the supplements and nutrients. Any person that decides not to eat meat can bear witness that it helps in the wellbeing of a person since they will eat more plant-based nourishments, and in light of the fact that they might be increasingly dynamic in settling on solid decisions.

A vegan diet lessens the danger of coronary illness, stoutness, type 2 diabetes hypertension, and a few kinds of malignancy, prompting a more extended future. It might prompt weight reduction. A veggie lover diet can give a wide assortment of energizing, nutritious nourishments. Various kinds of veggie lover eat various things.

- Lacto-ovo-vegans maintain a strategic distance from the substance with everything being equal.

- Pescatarians take fish, however, no meat

- Lacto-vegans expend dairy items however no eggs

- Ovo-veggie lovers devour eggs yet no dairy

- Vegans maintain a strategic distance from all creature-based nourishments, including nectar

A few people call themselves "semi-veggie lover," yet most veggie lover and vegetarian social orders don't acknowledge this term. A vegan needs to settle on cautious decisions about their eating regimen, to consume a wide assortment of nourishments to guarantee that they meet their healthful prerequisites. A few veggie lovers may need to take supplements. Delivering vegan nourishment is all the more naturally supportable, and it decreases harm to the earth. Numerous individuals quit eating meat for ideological, moral, or strict reasons. Fittingly arranged veggie-lover, including vegetarian, counts calories are healthfully satisfactory, and treat specific illnesses. These eating regimens are fitting for all phases of the existence cycle, including pregnancy, lactation, early stages, youth, youthfulness, more established adulthood, and for competitors.

A veggie lover diet ought to be a piece of an in general sound way of life, which incorporates practice and prohibits undesirable decisions, for example, smoking and drinking overabundance liquor. Individuals that do not consume meat may come up short on specific supplements.

Supplements that can be missing include:

- Calcium

- Iron

- Zinc

- Vitamin D

- Vitamin B12

- Protein

As nourishment descends the stomach related tract, signals are sent to the mind, and gut hormones are created that influence vitality balance in an assortment of ways, including easing back gastric discharging, going about as synapses, and diminishing gastrointestinal emissions. These impacts are proposed to impact satiety. The terms satiety and satiation are regularly utilized contrastingly in the writing and numerous strategies to quantify each exist.

Dissolvable filaments were considered to affect serum lipids, and insoluble strands were connected with laxation benefits. This division of solvent and insoluble fiber is as yet utilized in nourishment marking. Nonetheless, regardless of these ordinarily utilized speculations, logical proof supporting that solvent filaments lower cholesterol, and insoluble strands increment stool weight is conflicting. Numerous fiber sources are generally dissolvable yet at the same time grow stool weight, for example, oat grain and phylum. Additionally, dissolvable filaments, for example, inulin don't bring down blood lipids. Most foods grown from the ground are moved in insoluble fiber, not solvent fiber

Natural products have a high water substance and low levels of protein and fat. The protein is gathered in the seeds and is impervious to absorption in the small digestive tract and bacterial corruption in the internal organ. Organic products contain generally sugars and filaments, for example, gelatin, that are widely matured in the digestive organ. A few foods grown from the ground have been considered independently either in planned companion examines or randomized controlled preliminaries. Normally, these natural products or vegetables are of intrigue in view of their phytochemical substance, including polyphenols, phytoestrogens, and cancer prevention agents Cranberries have been considered all the more widely, particularly for their job in avoidance and treatment of urinary tract diseases

Potatoes are a staple vegetable in numerous pieces of the world. In contrast to verdant green vegetables, potatoes are wealthy in starch and give protein of high organic worth. Potatoes are plentiful in nutrient C and potassium and give dietary fiber, particularly if the skins are devoured. Glucose levels do influence satiety, and along these lines the admission of vitality as starch must be controlled and adjusted

The bioavailability of mixes in foods grown from the ground might be adjusted by the physical property of the natural product or vegetables, in spite of the fact that these cooperation's are hard to consider in the entire creature. Fiber is unquestionably a functioning segment of foods grown from the ground and motivation to keep on supporting their utilization.

Filaments, similar to starches, are made for the most part of many sugar units fortified together. Dissimilar to most starches, nonetheless, these bonds can't be separated by stomach related chemicals and pass generally flawless into the digestive organ. There, fiber can be aged by the colonic microflora to gases, for example, hydrogen and carbon dioxide, or it can go through the internal organ and tie water, expanding stool weight. In spite of the fact that strands are not changed over to glucose, some are delivered in the gut as filaments are aged.

Products of the soil are commonly low in vitality thickness and frequently are great wellsprings of fiber and potassium, yet the healthful commitment of standard servings of leafy foods shifts generally plant nourishments have just certain amino acids. So as to get a reasonable appropriation of basic amino acids, it was felt that common supplementation inside a dinner was required (for example, devouring vegetables, for example, beans, high in lysine content with grains, for example, rice.

Natural products, vegetables, and vegetables change broadly in supplement content, so ought not be relied upon to have comparative physiological impacts. Albeit dietary direction is strong of a more veggie lover eating design, including expanded servings of foods grown from the ground, the logical help for these suggestions is blended in a proof-based audit.

Supplements in leafy foods, for example, dietary fiber, nutrients, minerals, and phytochemicals, including polyphenols, all offer help for the natural believability that products of the soil assume a job in wellbeing. Nourishment structure may assume a job in satiety. Fiber added to drinks shows up less successful than entire organic products or vegetables in improving satiety. Admissions of foods grown from the ground are additionally generally advanced, both for the substance of fiber and different supplements.

CHAPTER 3:
THE TYPES OF FOOD TO AVOID

Our bodies and mind cooperate as one. It is thusly significant that we treat it that way. By nourishing our bodies with nutritious nourishment, it will likewise prompt have a superior working cerebrum and psyche, and we will look and feel extraordinary. On the off chance that we then again feed ourselves with unfortunate nourishment, we will feel worn out and languid and make it hard for us to do anything during the day. We have the decision to sustain our bodies with the correct supplements just as positive reasoning, and we can be in control to settle on a cognizant choice day by day to do as such. Individuals once in a while talk about the nourishments they hurl out, yet the theme of nourishment squander is getting much more consideration nowadays.

People have various wholesome and diet-related needs, contingent upon sexual orientation, age, prescriptions utilized, and analyzed conditions. It is essential to comprehend which nourishments and refreshments are protected and which could be an issue. It's similarly critical to realize how to design dinners utilizing safe nourishments and refreshments. Building a sound plate is simple when you make a big part of food on a served plate should consist of food that is naturally grown from the ground. It's additionally an incredible method to include ploughing, flavor, and surface in addition to nutrients, minerals, and fiber. This is stuffed in leafy foods that are low in calories and fat.

Huge numbers of us experience a day simply eating since "we need to eat." Not many really observe what they are eating and in the event that it is supporting their bodies or not. Eating unfortunate isn't just about putting on weight or not. What really occurs in our bodies over the long haul is the thing that issues as a less than stellar eating routine can prompt unmistakably more issues in the long haul just as negatively affect our brains. Great sustenance incorporates WHAT you eat just as HOW MUCH you eat of it. Our bodies resemble a vehicle. On the off chance that you put the correct kind of fuel into it just as the perfect sum, it will benefit you. In the event that you don't take care of it and put an inappropriate fuel in, you may cause more mischief than anything. We do need to devour an assortment of nourishment yet in the correct segments. Our bodies just need a specific measure of nourishment from every nutritional category every day so as to endure else it begins remunerating in different manners to attempt to compensate for what it needs.

Numerous nourishments and beverages bought at the market incorporate a date, which shows when it ought to be utilized or sold by. Since these dates allude to the item's quality, it doesn't really mean they ought to be tossed out.

- "Use by," "Best by" and "Best Before" dates are found on nourishments, for example, mustard, serving of mixed greens dressing and ketchup. These items generally don't should be refrigerated until opened. By and large, they are sheltered to eat past the date as long as they have been put away appropriately.

- "Sell by" dates are shown on short-lived nourishments, for example, meats and dairy items. It's conceivable these nourishments might be utilized a couple of days after that date, as long as they were put away at a sheltered temperature.

Practice Good Food Safety

- Don't chance eating or drinking whatever you think has ruined.

- Eat remains inside 3 to 4 days (or stop for up to 3 to 4 months).

- Test your sanitation information or see whether it's a great opportunity to hurl those nourishments by downloading the "Is My Food Safe" application or getting to the Food Keeper App on the web.

- Create perfect stockpiling conditions

- Store nourishments in the storeroom, so items with closing dates are forthcoming.

- Place nourishments that could ruin rapidly inside sight, for example, in the front of the fridge

Realize which products of the soil to store in the fridge. Some products will cause different products of the soil to mature rapidly, so they should be isolated. Also, others ought to be put away in a cool, dim, dry spot. At times, nourishments and drinks — even energizing food sources and refreshments — can have ominous associations with specific prescriptions. Coming to and keeping up a more advantageous weight adds to your general wellbeing and prosperity. Losing even a couple of pounds or counteracting further weight gain has medical advantages. Different approaches to diminish wellsprings of included sugars include: making or purchasing more advantageous variants of heated products, incorporating nourishments and beverages with included sugars less frequently, and eating or drinking littler sums.

Sugar is found normally in certain nourishments and beverages, similar to products of the soil, yet it is likewise added to a considerable lot of them. Included sugars give these things a sweet taste. Such a large number of calories from included sugars, and after some time, this may influence their weight and wellbeing. Numerous individuals consider treats the fundamental wellspring of included sugars, yet numerous nourishments and beverages may contain included sugars. For instance, improved beverages like customary soda pops, some organic product beverages, and caffeinated drinks are altogether wellsprings of included sugars. Make certain to search for nourishments and beverages that lack sugar recorded as the primary fixing. Different instances of sugars and wellsprings of included sugars include dark colored sugar, sucrose, or nectar white granulated sugar.

Wellsprings of included sugars regularly need supplements required for good wellbeing, while nourishments and beverages that contain characteristic wellsprings of sugar give supplements, similar to nutrients and minerals. For instance, organic products like strawberries are an incredible wellspring of nutrient C, and milk gives nutrients A and D and calcium. The issue is that a large number of us incorporate an excessive number of wellsprings of included sugars or eat and drink bigger sums than is prescribed. At the point when this occurs, there is less space for increasingly nutritious nourishments and beverages. Fructose is a characteristic sugar found in numerous nourishments like products of the soil. Fructose is additionally found in 'table sugar.' Long chains of fructose are called fractals and are found in specific vegetables, wheat, and different nourishments. Fructose is sweet and is regularly made into high fructose corn syrup, utilized in soda pops, and handled nourishments.

Why (limit) fructose in my eating routine?

- Fructose malabsorption is the point at which your body doesn't process or retain fructose well. This can cause swelling, stomach torment, queasiness, gas, and the runs.

- Hereditary fructose narrow mindedness is an exceptionally uncommon hereditary issue. This is the point at which the liver can't enable the body to separate fructose.

Side effects can be increasingly genuine. This issue requires something beyond restricting fructose.

Fructose is caught up in the small digestive tract in a few different ways. In the event that glucose is available in equivalent sums with fructose, the body ingests fructose better. Free fructose without coordinating glucose is retained all the more gradually, which may cause an annoyed stomach. The most widely recognized nourishment proteins that can cause narrow mindedness are bovine's milk protein and gluten from wheat. An altered end diet expels dairy and gluten and some other explicit nourishments that might be desired or eaten a great deal.

- Eliminate all dairy items, including milk, cream, cheddar, curds, yogurt, spread, dessert, and solidified yogurt.

- Eliminate gluten, staying away from any nourishments that contain wheat, spelt, kamut, oats, rye, grain, or malt. This is the most significant piece of the eating routine. Substitute with dark colored rice, millet, and buckwheat, quinoa, sans gluten flour items, or potatoes, custard, and arrowroot items.

Take out greasy meats like hamburger, pork, or veal. It is OK to eat the accompanying except if you realize that you are unfavorably susceptible or delicate to them: chicken, turkey, sheep, and cold-water fish, for example, salmon, mackerel, sardines, and halibut. Pick natural/unfenced sources where accessible.

- Avoid liquor and caffeine and all items that may contain these fixings (counting soft drinks, cold arrangements, and homegrown tinctures).

- Avoid nourishments containing yeast or nourishments that advance yeast abundance, including handled nourishments, refined sugars, cheeses, economically arranged toppings, peanuts, vinegar, and mixed drinks.

- Avoid straightforward sugars, for example, treat, desserts, and handled nourishments.

Stay away from any nourishment that has been ruined (counting overripe produce, or curds with shape, for instance). Maintain a strategic distance from nourishments that have been matured, aged, or cured while wellbeing is an essential spark for veggie lovers; some non-vegans refer to wellbeing as an essential purpose behind the consideration of creature items in their eating regimen. Veggie lovers think about the oversight of high fat, elevated cholesterol creature items to be solid, while numerous non-vegans accept that abstention from creature items prompts healthful insufficiencies. This worry is especially common among guardians, and it is intriguing to take note that even some veggie lover guardians have these worries for creating kids.

Numerous non-veggie lovers additionally guarantee an absence of enthusiasm for vegan slims down on the grounds that they trust it won't fulfill their own taste inclinations or explicit "desires." During center gatherings, for instance, HRC found that members generally felt that it is hard to surrender creature items due to either an energy for specific items (e.g., cheddar) or yearnings for other people, for example, meat. These inclinations can be solid to the point that they will keep a few buyers from thinking about vegetarianism, not to mention really attempting the eating routine. Identified with the thought of taste inclination is the present scarcity of great meat and dairy substitutes to assist veggie lovers with making up for these desires and inclinations. Albeit a few customers are happy to attempt these elective things, numerous others guarantee that they don't fill the void left by remembering creature items for the eating routine

The absolute most significant hindrance to vegetarianism among kids and youthful grown-ups is guardians. Youngsters and youthful grown-ups are adapted to pursue the instances of grown-ups in the family unit; when the guardians are non-veggie lover, kids are frequently completely ignorant of vegan alternatives. Indeed, even in situations where kids or young people express an enthusiasm for veggie lover slims down, they are regularly denied the decision by their folks because of the observation that vegetarianism is healthfully insufficient. Bother additionally turns into an issue when the youngster's favored eating routine strays from the family's essential eating regimen. All in all, kids and youthful grown-ups living inside non-veggie lover families are regularly uninformed of vegetarianism or precluded the choice from securing being vegan. While supporting vegan decisions to youngsters, it is in this manner basic to likewise address the worries of their folks.

Drinking a lot of liquor can mess wellbeing up just as damage. Liquor is additionally high in vitality, so you should drink less on the off chance that you have to get more fit. There is no "sheltered" level of liquor for all individuals consistently. The sum you can drink relies upon your age, regardless of whether you are male or female, and your body size, nourishment admission, and general wellbeing. Removing creature items doesn't need to be a win big or bust recommendation. For some individuals, the ideal approach to change how they eat is to do it steadily. Eating plant-based nourishments a couple of days seven days, or for a specific segment of consistently (like before 6 p.m.) is an extraordinary method to rehearse your new propensity without being impeccable. Despite the fact that jettisoning meat has immense favorable circumstances for your wellbeing, it's conceivable to be a "shoddy nourishment vegan." After all, cake treats and potato chips would all be able to be made without creature items! While it's fine to enjoy now and then, kindly don't live off of French fries and pop. Be certain you're getting a lot of vegetables, natural products, beans, and entire grains in your eating regimen.

While fat, sugar, and salt can make nourishment taste incredible, it's best not to expend excessively. Swap margarine for a lower-fat spread, and pick low salt choices when purchasing flavoring like stock solid shapes. Bubbling or flame broiling nourishment is more beneficial than and similarly as scrumptious as searing with oil. An incidental treat of dessert, cakes, and desserts is something we as a whole love – however it merits recalling that they can contain loads of sugar and fat.

CHAPTER 4:
THE BASICS OF A PLANT-BASED MEAL

The objective of each diet ought to make a positive impact on the general wellbeing of the consumer. In this segment, we will survey the advantages of plant-based eating regimens. Individuals once in a while talk about the nourishments they hurl out, yet the point of nourishment squander is getting much more consideration nowadays. Veggie lover diets might be good in the loos of excess fats and have more nutritional values. By eating food that does not have meat one is able to achieve more nutrients. In spite of these little contrasts, there is proof that a comprehensively characterized plant-based eating routine has huge medical advantages. It ought to be noticed that the term plant-based is here and there utilized reciprocally with veggie lover or vegetarian. Veggie lover or vegetarian consumes fewer calories received for moral or strict reasons could conceivably be sound. It is, in this way, imperative to know the particular meanings of related weight control plans and to find out the subtleties of a patient's eating routine as opposed to making suspicions about how sound it is.

Regardless of the solid assortment of proof favoring plant-based counts calories, including examines indicating an eagerness of the overall population to grasp them, numerous doctors are not focusing on the significance of plant-based consumes less calories as a first-line treatment for constant diseases. This could be a direct result of an absence of consciousness of these eating regimens or an absence of patient training assets. Our bodies and mind cooperate as one. It is in this way significant that we treat it that way. By encouraging our bodies with nutritious nourishment, it will likewise prompt having a superior working cerebrum and brain, and we will look and feel incredible. On the off chance that we then again feed ourselves with unfortunate nourishment, we will feel worn out and lazy and make it hard for us to do anything during the day. We have the decision to bolster our bodies with the correct supplements just as positive reasoning, and we can be in control to settle on a cognizant choice day by day to do as such. People have various wholesome and diet-related needs, contingent upon sex, age, prescriptions utilized, and analyzed conditions. It is critical to comprehend which nourishments and refreshments are protected and which could be an issue. It's similarly essential to realize how to design dinners utilizing safe nourishments and drinks.

A sound, plant-based diet expects to utilize of supplement thick nourishments while limiting prepared nourishments, oils, and creature food. It empowers loads of vegetables natural products, beans, nuts, and soybeans (in littler sums) and is commonly not fatty. Building a solid plate is simple when you make a wide area of the food servings should be comprised of vegetables. It's likewise an extraordinary method to include shading, flavor, and surface in addition to nutrients, minerals, and fiber. This is stuffed in foods grown from the ground that are low in calories and fat. Individuals once in a while talk about the nourishments they hurl out, yet the point of nourishment squander is getting significantly more consideration nowadays. A significant number of us experience a day simply eating since "we need to eat." Not very many really observe what they are eating and in the event that it is feeding to their bodies or not. Eating undesirable isn't just about putting on weight or not. What really occurs in our bodies over the long haul is the thing that issues as a horrible eating routine can prompt undeniably more issues in the long haul just as negatively affect our brains. Great nourishment incorporates what you eat just as how much you eat of it. Our bodies resemble a vehicle. On the off chance that you put the correct kind of fuel into it just as the perfect sum, it will benefit you. In the event that you don't care for it and put an inappropriate fuel in, you may cause more mischief than anything. We do need to devour an assortment of nourishment yet in the correct segments. Our bodies just need a specific measure of nourishment from every nutrition class every day so as to endure else it begins repaying in different manners to attempt to compensate for what it needs.

Realize which products of the soil to store in the icebox. Some products will cause different foods grown from the ground to age rapidly, so they should be isolated. What's more, others ought to be put away in a cool, dim, dry spot. Now and again, nourishments and refreshments—even restorative food sources and drinks—can have negative collaborations with specific meds. Coming to and keeping up a more advantageous weight adds to your general wellbeing and prosperity. Losing even a couple of pounds or averting further weight gain has medical advantages. Different approaches to decrease wellsprings of included sugars include: making or purchasing more beneficial renditions of prepared products, incorporating nourishments and beverages with included sugars less frequently, and eating or drinking littler sums. Sugar is found normally in certain nourishments and beverages, similar to grown foods of the ground, yet it is likewise added to a large number of them.

Included sugars give these things a sweet taste. An excessive number of calories from included sugars, and after some time this may influence their weight and wellbeing. Numerous individuals consider treats the fundamental wellspring of included sugars, yet numerous nourishments and beverages may contain included sugars. For instance, improved beverages like standard soda pops, some natural product beverages, and caffeinated drinks are for the most part wellsprings of included sugars.

Make certain to search for nourishments and beverages that don't have sugar (or some other sugar) recorded as the principal fixing. Different instances of sugars and wellsprings of included sugars include high-fructose corn syrup, nectar, maple syrup, molasses, and white granulated sugar. Wellsprings of included sugars regularly need supplements required for good wellbeing, while nourishments and beverages that contain characteristic wellsprings of sugar give supplements, similar to nutrients and minerals. For instance, organic products like strawberries are an extraordinary wellspring of nutrient C, and milk gives nutrients D and A and calcium. The issue is that a considerable lot of us incorporate such a large number of wellsprings of included sugars or eat and drink bigger sums than is prescribed. At the point when this occurs there is less space for increasingly nutritious nourishments and beverages. Fructose is a characteristic sugar found in numerous nourishments like products of the soil. Fructose is likewise found in 'table sugar.' Long chains of fructose are called fructans and are found in specific vegetables, wheat, and different nourishments. Fructose is extremely sweet and is frequently made into high fructose corn syrup, utilized in soda pops, and prepared nourishments.

People eating plant-based foods have been related to an assortment of medical advantages, including sound weight, ideal wellbeing, and life span. Well-arranged vegan eats less are totally fortifying and healthfully sufficient for individuals all through all phases of life and that they have various wellbeing focal points, including lower danger of coronary illness, lower circulatory strain levels, and lower danger of hypertension and type 2 diabetes. What's more, veggie lovers will, in general, have a lower body weight and lower by and large disease rates, lower admissions of fat and cholesterol, potassium, nutrients C and E, flavonoids, and different phytochemicals. Veggie lovers, vegans, and omnivores comprehend the advantages of receiving entire nourishments, plant-based eating systems. All meat isn't made equivalent. Sheep, meat, pork, and cheddar produce the most ozone harming substances. They additionally will, in general, be high in fat and have the most exceedingly awful ecological effects. Veggie lover style eating designs have been related with improved wellbeing results, including lower levels of corpulence, a decreased danger of cardiovascular ailment, lower circulatory strain, and lower all out mortality.

Expanding proof fiber-rich, plant-based eating regimen advances solid gut smaller scale biota, connected to safe help and stomach related wellbeing. Like most things throughout everyday life, moving to a completely plant-based diet is an adventure. In the event that you are accustomed to eating meat, you can begin by chopping down, so you are following a to a great extent vegan-based eating routine yet every so often still eat meat – this is known as flexitarianism. Whatever your explanation behind eliminating your meat utilization, even a small decrease will have a constructive outcome. Following a full veggie lover diet avoids all meat, fish, poultry, and fish – so a vegan diet will concentrate on grains, beats, nuts, seeds, products of the soil. Most veggie lovers still incorporate dairy and eggs. A plant-based diet prohibits meat, fish, poultry, fish, dairy, and eggs – a few people additionally decide to refuse items, for example, nectar. A considerable lot of those following a plant-based diet may likewise decide to maintain a strategic distance from other non-nourishment creature items, for example, calfskin or beeswax. eating less meat and dairy – or in any event, removing it by and large - will positively affect your wellbeing, on creature welfare, and on nature.

Regardless of in case you're a grown-up shopping for food for your family or a high school eating in a cafeteria - you can at present live your qualities and vote with your fork. Eating eggs as well as dairy? Get them from the nearby, little peaceful ranch. Eating meat? Get it from ranchers who approach animals with deference and advance manageable horticulture. Tell the supermarket and cafeteria chief what sort of items you need to purchase. Each decision matters. The prosperity of my kindred human is the thing that moves me to purchase natural, nearby, and reasonable exchange. I don't purchase natural/reasonable exchange since, over succulent legacy tomatoes, I do it, so our grandchildren have prolific soil staying to develop nourishment in, better wages for workers, and to open ranch laborers to less pesticides. At the point when I eat less meat, it implies I am requesting fewer creatures be sent through the way toward being raised for nourishment. Which means I'm oppressing less of my kindred people from working with creatures such that I wouldn't do myself. Anybody with access to an assortment of nourishments will get a scope of all the fundamental amino acids they need. I'll even go the extent that platitude it's difficult to make a 100% plant-based eating regimen that is protein lacking as long as the accompanying three prerequisites are met:

1. You manufacture an eating regimen around an assortment of nourishments (e.g., vegetables, beans, grains, natural products, nuts, and seeds) some plant-put together diets are overwhelming with respect to starch-thick nourishments (e.g., pasta, potatoes, and oat) and organic products. Starch-thick nourishments and organic products are fine, taste great, and give supplements.... yet you should abstain from giving them a chance to be the establishment of your eating regimen. On the off chance that you assemble you're eating routine around just starch-thick nourishments and organic products, you may run into protein and fat lack issues, alongside getting an abundance of sugars. Same thought goes on the off chance that somebody depends just on nuts/seeds to address protein issues. They will get an excess of fat. It's about extents and equalization.

2. You eat enough nourishment to continue a sound body size when we meet our vitality (calorie) needs; protein can do what it needs to do in the body. Notwithstanding,

without enough nourishment coming in every day, protein is redirected to different capacities in the body that it isn't perfect for, such as creating vitality. On the off chance that you don't eat enough nourishment, you may become protein insufficient, yet everything lacking.

3. You incorporate in any event 1 cup of cooked vegetables every day Closer to 1 ½ cups on the off chance that you are greater, more like 1 cup on the off chance that you are littler. Do this with whatever supper you like, or spread it for the duration of the day. Beans/vegetables are underutilized by practically everyone. In any case, beans are the new meat! Where you recently ate some meat, having a go at substituting a few vegetables. (For sustenance geeks: Legumes are a rich wellspring of lysine, and in the event that somebody eating plant-based is going to miss the mark in one of the amino acids, lysine is most likely the one.)

A few people guarantee that enemy of supplement mixes like lectins and phytic corrosive in beans and entire grains merit keeping away from. This is what we have to recollect: These sorts of mixes are broadly appropriated in nourishment things normally devoured by people and have been for a long time. Most of nourishment specialists accept they don't represent a hazard to human wellbeing. At last, in case you're eating a plant-based eating regimen and have affirmed supplement insufficiencies, and you've attempted all the above procedures with no achievement, including modest quantities of creature nourishments every so often may support stores of vital minerals in your body. You aren't an ethical disappointment in the event that you do this. Furthermore, you can even pick animal items from ranchers who are doing great on the planet! Trial with finding a negligible degree of creature nourishment admission that supports your wellbeing needs. Keep in mind; all nourishments have advantages and disadvantages. Indeed, kale and cabbage are nutritious, AND these cruciferous veggies can likewise aggregate substantial metals, and other tricky exacerbates that can hinder typical real procedures (e.g., generation of thyroid hormones). Along these lines, if those are the ONLY vegetables you eat, you may begin to feel terrible. This applies to all nutrition classes. For instance, on the off chance that you are as of now ONLY eating nutty spread, attempt to turn with cashew margarine, sunflower seed margarine, and almond margarine. On the off chance that you are as of now ONLY eating soy, attempt to turn with lentils, split peas, and aduki beans. In the event that you are as of now ONLY eating wheat, attempt to turn with spelled, amaranth, and buckwheat. You get the thought. Now and then eating an increasingly occasional eating routine can help normally sign a rotational methodology

A few people can't change over plant carotenoids into the dynamic type of nutrient A. So, while it may show up they are expending enough nutrients on paper, the body truly isn't getting a usable structure. This is one of those interesting distinction things. You may improve expending some preformed nutrients (called retinol, found in creature nourishments and enhancements). While apparently individuals can blossom with a 100% plant-based eating regimen, this supposition is made dependent on our present comprehension of sustenance. Furthermore, our present comprehension is restricted. We don't have the foggiest idea about the entirety of the different mixes and supplements that exist in nourishments. On the off chance that you find that you improve remembering some creature items for your eating routine, incorporate them. Expect to locate that insignificant powerful portion. Possibly a couple of others consciously raised eggs every week. Some neighborhood/natural yogurt each other day. Some field raised meat every month. Keep in mind, the best thing you can accomplish for your wellbeing is to know yourself. The following best stuff to achieve is to satisfy your gut feelings.

CHAPTER 5:
THE BENEFITS OF PLANT-BASED MEALS TO OUR BODY.

A progressively feasible future requires making a move to guarantee more advantageous nourishment rehearses in human services offices. Nourishment is a focal part of our lives - in addition to the fact that it provides basic sustenance, it assumes a principal job in the economy and is installed in social personalities. The nourishment we produce, devour and squander, be that as it may, likewise impact sly affects human wellbeing and the earth. "Plant-based" is additionally a trendy expression we see to an ever-increasing extent. However, what precisely is a plant-based eating routine and what makes it solid? Going plant-based would one say one is of the best things you can accomplish for your wellbeing and the health of creatures all over, yet you likely definitely realized that, correct? You may definitely realize that eating a plant-based eating regimen is solid.

There is a developing development towards implanting atmosphere well-disposed practices in numerous areas of society; the human services part has a one of a kind chance to ensure natural and general wellbeing, which can be accomplished by executing economic nourishment rehearses in medicinal services offices. A plant-based diet implies eating all the more entire nourishments and plants-natural stuff such as grains, seeds, and vegetables. Probably the best part about eating a plant-based eating routine is that you can characterize your severity. It doesn't really mean plants as it were. For around, a plant-based eating plan excludes every single creature item (a vegetarian diet). For other people, it's just about extent picking a greater amount of your nourishments from plant sources. It's a decent method to make plants a principle part of your eating regimen without expecting to totally dispense with dairy and meat. Plants are great, and the greater part of us don't eat the suggested measure of foods grown from the ground, so making most of your eating plans plant-based will up your produce bet, which is a nutritious decision. Leafy foods are plentiful in nutrients, minerals, cancer prevention agents and fiber. Fiber is a supplement that a large portion doesn't get the best of, and it has huge amounts of solid advantages it useful for your waistline, your heart, your gut, and your glucose. Be that as it may, likewise, science shows that individuals' general nourishment is normally better when they pursue a veggie diet versus an omnivorous eating routine.

Individuals who pursue a plant-based eating regimen will, in general, have lower weight files (BMIs) contrasted with their omnivore partners. What's more, look into shows that individuals who utilize a veggie-lover diet to get in shape are progressively effective at dropping pounds. Eating a veggie-lover diet may bring down your danger of cardiovascular ailment, and may improve other hazard factors for coronary illness by bringing down your circulatory strain and cholesterol, and improving your glucose control. Consuming a plant-based diet can likewise help suppress irritation, which raises your danger of coronary illness by advancing plaque development in your courses. Despite your BMI, eating a veggie lover diet or a vegetarian diet brings down your danger of diabetes. Indeed, one investigation shows that meat-eaters have twofold the danger of diabetes contrasted with lacto ovo-veggie lovers and vegetarians. Research reliably shows that routinely eating a lot of natural products, veggies, vegetables and grains-otherwise known as plants-is related with a lower malignancy chance. In addition, those infection battling phytochemicals in plants have additionally been appeared to forestall and obstruct malignant growth. Furthermore, remember, contemplates additionally show a relationship between eating red and prepared meats and expanded disease hazard, particularly colorectal malignant growth. So there's advantage from simply eating more plants, yet in addition from supplanting some less-solid nourishments with those plant food sources. You can and ought to up your vegetable bet plan to ensure half of your lunch and supper plate is constantly loaded up with vegetables, and change the assortment and shade of the veggies you pick.

Good Sleep

A plant-based food is extraordinarily useful for your rest wellbeing. Despite the fact that you'll likely have unlimited measures of vitality for a duration, you'll likely be more quiet and think that it's simpler to fall asleep to rest. In addition, certain nourishments like sweet potatoes, cashew spread, avocados, kale, pecans, spinach, and squash all have nutrient B6, tryptophan which guarantee a solid rest cycle. Kales, strengthened portions of dried figs and almond are likewise more extravagant in calcium than milk

Minimal Inflammation

Have join torment? Make sure to eat lots of vegetables! The nourishments lower aggravation. Particularly those wealthy in omega-3 fats such as chia seeds, alongside verdant greens with chlorophyll, which assuages irritation. Eating a plant-based meal plan helps builds alkalinity in the body to quiet aggravation. An eating regimen high in creature nourishments advances corrosiveness, which can prompt everything from joint pain to gout to incessant stomach irritation.

Search out sound fats.

Fats that are unsaturated and polyunsaturated are useful for your heart. A large portion of the great nourishment wellsprings of these originate from olive oil, avocado, and its oil, nuts, and oils. Substitute these every so often (or consistently, on the off chance that you like) for spread, ghee, or grease, and you're consequently inclining toward more plants. Expect to incorporate plant wellsprings of omega-3 unsaturated fats as well, for example, flaxseeds and chia seeds.

More Energy

Creature nourishments are incredibly difficult to process. At the point when the stomach related framework becomes overpowered, it is capable of taking away all the vitality from you. Consuming more vegetables eating regimen is an incredible method to upgrade your vitality since absorption is normally simpler and a couple of more plant-based nourishments have stimulating capabilities. Simply know about segment size since eating incredibly enormous suppers can likewise be burdening on your framework.

Have a vegan supper once every week.

Generally, we put a creature protein at the focal point of the plate at dinnertime, so going vegan one day seven days is one approach to reduce. Furthermore, in light of the fact that it's only one supper, it doesn't require some other speculation through the span of the week. On the off chance that going without meat for a feast feels like a stretch, at that point move your observation and check whether you can make creature protein to a greater extent a topping than a stay to your dinner one night seven days.

Better Digestion

Vegetables nourishments are fundamentally fiber, sound fats, and water, vegetable protein. Nothing in those nourishments (except if you pick profoundly handled variants) that reason you're processing to back off or stand firm still. Simply remember that the additional admission of fiber ought to be grasped with alert. Go slowly and bite your nourishment quite well, which likewise improves the absorption procedure. For the individuals who devour a ton of milk, cheddar, and meat, this is probably the best change you can make for mending ceaseless clogging, gas, swelling, stomach irritation, and acid reflux.

Attempt one new-to-you plant nourishment seven days.

In the event that this is your objective, you're not simply expanding the measure of plants you're eating, but at the same time, you're changing up your eating routine, which implies you'll be getting an alternate equalization of bravo nutrients and minerals. Some less-normal veggies to attempt bok choy, rutabaga, squash blooms, celeriac, kohlrabi.

Pretty Skin

Your skin will look staggering following seven days of a vegetable only eating regimen. Vegetables with nourishments are plentiful in nutrient A, nutrient C, cancer prevention agents like chlorophyll, water, and vitamin E, which all accomplish astounding things for your skin. The absolute best wagers are avocado, apples, oranges, greens, broccoli, sweet potatoes, lemons, beets, squash, and tomatoes.

Have vegetables at breakfast.

On the off chance that you need to build your veggie consumption, start with breakfast. Since it is anything but a dinner you'd, for the most part, consider as veggie-filled, including some here, makes it simpler to hit your everyday quantity. At that point keep lunch and supper in its present condition. In case you're thinking about what veggie-substantial morning meals may resemble, have a go at adding spinach to your eggs, mixing cauliflower in your smoothie, or having a morning meal plate of mixed greens.

More joyful look

When you eat in a way that improves your lifestyle, you become more joyful. Your point of view will become positive and become an all-round happy person. Numerous individuals do not see this change coming, but they finally come to terms with the result of eating more vegetables.

Attempt natural product for pastries and tidbits.

Sweet is regularly something made with a creature item margarine or eggs, or both, in treats, cakes, and frozen yogurt. Exchanging over to natural product now and again can fulfill your sweet tooth with an entire nourishment, and furthermore give you an additional serving of plants.

Better Blood Sugar

A plant-based diet hinders glucose, yet still enables insulin to carry out its responsibility inside the cells. The vast majority discover they don't endure low glucose, hypoglycemia, or some other manifestations of diabetes inside seven days of a plant-based eating regimen. You'll likely receive rewards from eliminating meat (plant nourishments have less immersed fat and typically less calories). However, it goes past what you're restricting. What you're eating and adding to your eating regimen is noteworthy, as well. Eating more plants implies getting a greater amount of those bravo nutrients, minerals, phytochemicals and fiber-a significant number of which are supplements we regularly miss the mark on.

A plant-based diet has overwhelmingly demonstrated diminished danger of Ovarian, Cervix, Prostate, Digestive Tract, Lung, and Bladder malignant growth, and in all cases included a critical guide in inversion of such tumors with customary drug. Surveys of different investigations that took a gander at the wellbeing results of vegans and individuals who eat meat announced a significant discovering: veggie lovers have altogether lower paces of malignancy. This incorporates malignant growths of different kinds. A single study found that veggie lovers charge stunningly better. For every one of the reasons that veggie lover and vegan diets can decrease malignancy chances, these eating regimens are useful for disease patients.

Numerous individuals grow up believing that creature items like meat and milk are fundamental parts of a sound diet. Nonetheless, well-arranged veggie-lover counts calories pursue good dieting rules and contains every one of the supplements that our bodies need. Another putative robotic pathway of how plant-based diets can influence wellbeing may include the gut micro biome, which has progressively gotten logical and prevalent intrigue. Besides, it has been presented that the microbiome may impact real homeostatic control, recommending a job for the gut microbiota in entire body control instruments on the foundational level. The microbiota to a great extent adds to synapse forerunner focuses; in this manner, notwithstanding estimating synapse antecedents in the serum, metabolomics on fecal examples would be useful to additionally comprehend the utilitarian job of the gut microbiota in synapse biosynthesis and guideline Showing the significance of gut microbiota for perception, a first human examination evaluating subjective tests and cerebrum imaging could recognize corpulent from no obese people utilizing a microbial profile. Probiotics could upgrade intellectual capacity in solid subjects, indicating little impacts on improved memory execution and diminished feelings of anxiety. There is a general hearty help for gainful impacts of a plant-put together diet with respect to metabolic measures in wellbeing and sickness.

A plant-based diet with low fat or very little meat may actually help avoid and or in other ways, treat diabetes, perhaps by making better the insulin levels to affect and diminishing insulin obstruction. A plant-based diet can impact cerebrum work by still misty fundamental instruments of a modified microbial status and foundational metabolic adjustments. Plant-based eating regimens may offer a preferred position over those that are not plant-based regarding anticipation and the executives of diabetes.

Vegetables weight control plans were related to a decreased danger of heart illness and death contrasted and meat and animal products eating regimens. The advantage of plant-put together diets with respect to mortality might be essentially brought about by diminished utilization of red meat. Maintaining a strategic distance from over the top utilization of meat, which is related to an expanded danger of so much cause of deaths and an expanded danger of heart mortality. Minor consuming of meat consumption has been related to life span.

All things considered, people that eat a lot of vegetables are far not at the risk of running low in terms of protein deficiency. Proteins are stored in the form of amino acids, which are very essentials acids in the body and which the body has to outsource as it cannot make its own amino acids. Vital amino acids are basically found in meat products, cow products, and bird products, too similarly the same number of plant-based sustenance's. Important acids that are required in the body are able to be gotten by one eating a mixture of a number of plants. Models consolidate dim hued rice and beans, with wheat pita. In like manner, a composed, plant-based eating routine will give adequate proportions of basic amino acids and foresee protein deficiency. Soybeans and sustenance are created utilizing soybeans are incredible wellsprings of protein and may help lower levels of low-thickness lipoprotein in the blood and diminish the peril of hip splits and a couple of dangerous developments. Plant-based weight control plans are made up of iron, but this same iron is found in vegetables but a bit different from the meat one in structure.

Calcium confirmation can be palatable in a composed, meticulously orchestrated, plant-based eating routine. People who don't eat plants that contain high proportions of calcium may be in peril for debilitated bone mineralization and breaks. In any case, contemplates have exhibited that break peril was near for veggie darlings and non-vegans. The best approach to prosperity of the bone is palatable calcium affirmation, which is available apparently, to be autonomous of eating tendencies. Some immense wellsprings of vitamins fuse found in kale, tofu, bok choy, and mustard. Some greens such as spinach and other various plants have calcium that, and turnip greens, yet bountiful, is useful to oxalate and along these lines is insufficiently devoured. Plant-based things, for instance, soy milk and oat grains, may be strengthened to give an adequate wellspring of Vitamin D.

A sound, plant-based diet requires orchestrating, getting imprints, and request. The recommendations for sick people that require a vegetable-only feeding routine can get all that they require by combining nuts, beans, vegetables, all greens, and seeds. Thus keeping up a vital good ways and reducing intake of animal products that include: oils, sugars, fats, etc. people that start a vegetable-only eating routine use little or no medication for weight issues and have a lessened threat of dangerous development, and an abatement in their risk of death from ischemic coronary ailment. A plant-based diet isn't a success enormous or bust program, anyway a way of life that is custom-fitted to each individual. It may be especially productive for those with heaviness, Type 2 diabetes, hypertension, lipid issue, or cardiovascular infirmity. The points of interest recognized will be similar to the level of adherence, and the proportion of animal things ate up. Demanding kinds of plant-based keeps away from nourishment with for all intents and purposes zero animal things may be required for individuals with inoperable or genuine coronary course disease. Low-sodium, plant-based diets may be supported for individuals with hypertension or a family heritage of coronary supply course infirmity or stroke. Sick people with diabetes and weight issues are most likely going to benefit from a vegetable-only diet with a moderate proportion of nourishments developed from the beginning irrelevant low-fat animal products. Genuine power requires organization and coordination that work together with a low-calorie meal and the supervision of a specialist's gathering. People that are suffering from kidney problems need a vegetable-only feeding routine with remarkable restrictions; for example, nourishments developed starting from the earliest stage are potassium-rich and phosphorus-rich too.

CHAPTER 6:
A CHEAT DAY

A more sustainable future requires taking action to ensure healthier food practices in healthcare facilities. Food is a central component of our lives - not only does it provide essential nourishment; it plays a fundamental role in the economy and is embedded in cultural identities. The food we produce, consume, and waste, however, also has major impacts on human health and the environment. Eating "plant-based" sounds solid. What's more, it is. "Plant-based" is likewise a popular expression we see to an ever-increasing extent. In any case, what precisely is a plant-based eating routine and what makes it sound? Going plant-based would one say one is of the best things you can accomplish for your wellbeing and the health of creatures all over the place, yet you likely definitely realized that, correct? You may definitely realize that vegetable only eating routine is sound and pure for nature. You do realize a few immediate, explicit advantages you may understanding inside the major principal seven-day rule plan of eating vegetables. You may find this interesting to even thinking of giving it a try. There is a developing development towards implanting atmosphere benevolent practices in numerous segments of society; the human services segment has a novel chance to ensure natural and general wellbeing, which can be accomplished by actualizing manageable nourishment rehearses in medicinal services offices.

A plant-based diet implies eating all the more entire nourishments and plants-organic products, vegetables, entire grains, vegetables, and nuts, and seeds. Perhaps the best part about eating a plant-based eating routine is that you can characterize your severity. It doesn't really mean plants as it were. For somewhere in the range of, a plant-based eating routine excludes every creature item (a vegetarian diet). For other people, it's just about extent picking a greater amount of your nourishments from plant sources than from creature sources. It's a pleasant method to make plants a principle part of your eating routine without expecting to totally take out dairy, eggs, meat, and fish. Plants are solid. You know this-and a large portion of us don't eat the suggested measure of foods grown from the ground, so making most of your eating routine plant-based will up your produce risk, which is a nutritious decision. Foods grown from the ground are plentiful in nutrients, minerals, cancer prevention agents and fiber. Fiber is a supplement that a large portion of us don't get enough of, and it has huge amounts of solid advantages it useful for your waistline, your heart, your gut, and your glucose. However, likewise, science shows that individuals' general sustenance is normally better when they pursue a veggie lover or vegetarian diet versus when they eat an omnivorous eating routine. Individuals who pursue a plant-based eating regimen will, in general, have lower weight lists (BMIs) contrasted with their omnivore partners. Furthermore, look into shows that individuals who utilize a veggie-lover diet to get in shape are progressively effective at dropping pounds, yet in addition to keeping them off.

Eating a veggie-lover diet may bring down your danger of cardiovascular infection, and may improve other hazard factors for coronary illness by bringing down your circulatory strain and cholesterol, and improving your glucose control. Eating plant-based can likewise help control aggravation, which raises your danger of coronary illness by advancing plaque development in your veins. Despite your BMI, eating a veggie lover diet or a vegetarian diet brings down your danger of diabetes. Indeed, one investigation shows that meat-eaters have twofold the danger of diabetes contrasted with lacto ovo-veggie lovers and vegetarians. Research reliably shows that routinely eating a lot of organic products, veggies, vegetables, and grains-otherwise known as plants-is related with a lower malignancy hazard. In addition, those sickness battling phytochemicals in plants have additionally been appeared to counteract and frustrate malignancy. What's more, remember, considers likewise show a relationship between eating red and handled meats and expanded disease hazard, particularly colorectal malignant growth. So there's advantage from simply eating more plants, yet in addition from supplanting some less-solid nourishments with those plant food sources. You can and ought to up your vegetable risk intend to ensure half of your lunch and supper plate is constantly loaded up with vegetables, and fluctuate the assortment and shade of the veggies you pick.

Sleeping better

After consuming a lot of vegetables for dinner, you get to see that it is amazing how you will sleep well at night. Despite the fact that you will most likely have unlimited measures of vitality for the duration of daytime and you will most definitely feel very peaceful and think that it is simpler to fall asleep so as to rest. Furthermore, some certain kinds of nourishments like sweet potatoes, spinach, broccoli, avocados, mustard nutty spread, bananas, kale, almonds, cashew margarine pecans, and squash all contain nutrient B6, tryptophan, and magnesium, which guarantee a sound rest cycle.

Reduced swelling

Do you feel any kind of pain in the joints? If so, then you really need to consume a lot of different kinds of vegetables. They will assist in cooling or calming down the pain, particularly those vegetables that have more of the useful fats and nutrients that are embedded in chlorophyll and go into the body and also assist it in relaxing the pains they might be experiencing. Consuming a lot of vegetables gives the body an alkaline pH setting that is able to help the body to fight the irritation it might be experiencing. An eating regimen high in creature nourishments advances causticity which can prompt everything from joint inflammation to gout to constant stomach irritation.

Search out solid fats.

Unsaturated fats-monounsaturated and polyunsaturated-are the thoughtful that are useful for your heart. The vast majority of the great nourishment wellsprings of these originate from plants-olives and olive oil, avocado, and its oil, nuts, and their margarines and oils. Substitute these periodically (or consistently, on the off chance that you like) for spread, ghee, or grease, and you're naturally inclining toward more plants. Expect to incorporate plant wellsprings of omega-3 unsaturated fats as well, for example, flaxseeds and chia seeds.

More Energy.

Creature nourishments are very difficult for the body to process. At the point when the stomach related framework becomes overpowered, it takes away all the vitality directly in your direction. A vegetable eating routine is an extraordinary method to improve your vitality since absorption is normally simpler, and various vegetable nourishments contain empowering properties. Simply know about segment size since eating amazingly enormous suppers can likewise be burdening on your framework.

Have a veggie-lover supper once per week.

Normally we put a creature protein at the focal point of the plate at dinnertime, so going veggie lover one day seven days is one approach to reduce. What's more, since it's only one supper, it doesn't require some other venture through the span of the week. In the event that is going sans meat for dinner feels like a stretch, at that point move your observation and check whether you can make creature protein to a greater degree a fixing than a stay to your supper one night seven days.

Better Digestion.

Vegetables nutrients can be classified as the following: fats, fiber, proteins, and water. Everything in the nutrients (except if you pick profoundly handled forms) that reason your processing to back off or stand firm still. Simply remember that the additional admission of fiber ought to be grasped with alert. Move slowly and bite your nourishment well indeed, which likewise upgrades the absorption procedure. For the individuals who expend a great deal of dairy products, cheddar, and animal products, this is probably the perfect decision you can make for recuperating interminable clogging, swelling, abdominal aggravation, and acid reflux.

Attempt one new-to-you plant nourishment seven days.

On the off chance that this is your objective, you're not simply expanding the measure of plants you're eating, but at the same time, you are to change up your eating routine, which implies you will be getting an alternate equalization of bravo nutrients and minerals. Some less-normal veggies to attempt bok choy, rutabaga, squash blooms, celeriac, kohlrabi.

With the numerous weight control plans, it is normal to incorporate a "cheat day" or "cheat feast" about once every week. It can assist you with enduring the confinements for the remainder of the time. In any case, there is discussion about whether this applies to veganism in light of the fact that being vegetarian is regularly founded on moral standards.

It is practically difficult to stay with a solid eating routine in 100% of your time. The inclination to eat something outside our endorsed eating regimen once gets everybody. In any case, on the off chance that you get back on the way of eating undesirable suppers brimming with many calories, your wellness objectives can immediately turn into a relic of days gone by. In this manner, numerous specialists prescribe not dodging these allurements in your eating routine; however, including a cheat supper or cheat day in your eating regimen plan. While picking the correct routine can be extremely intense, regularly the greatest weight reduction challenge is making and adhering to new propensities that help your wellbeing or weight reduction objectives without passing up the nourishments that you love. Cheat days are very famous among wellness aficionados. You adhere to an exacting eating regimen for the entire week, with the exception of just one day when you let yourself eat whatever your heart wants or a certain food that you might be craving to eat. The consolidation of cheat dinners or cheat days into an eating routine arrangement has been prevalent among wellness aficionados for quite a while. However, it's currently advancing into standard eating regimen culture by method for internet-based life. Conning inside an eating regimen plan includes giving yourself determined, arranged authorization to incidentally disrupt exacting eating routine norms.

Cheat days: Eating pizza for breakfast, drinking frozen yogurt for lunch, and may a hamburger or even some French fries for supper? On a cheat day, it is the only time that you are permitted to eat anything that you desire. What this day resembles depends altogether on you: some eat up all that they can get their hands on. It's conceivable that you may devour twice the same number of calories as on a typical day. Others pick a less outrageous form and increment their day by day calorie admission with solid, fatty nourishments. The hypothesis behind this reward-based eating routine methodology is that by permitting yourself brief times of guilty pleasure, you'll be bound to adhere to your recommended eating routine most of the time. When utilizing the cheat procedure, individuals will commonly utilize either a cheat supper or cheat day approach. As the names suggest, a cheat supper is a solitary dinner that veers from your arranged eating regimen design, while a cheat day takes into consideration free nourishment decisions for a whole day. A cheat dinner or a cheat day can help renew your glycogen stores by expanding the quantity of calories and starches you are devouring. This can give you the vitality your requirement for a strenuous exercise; however, going over the edge on your cheat day can, obviously, likewise set you back a piece with your weight reduction objectives. Cheat diet strategies are profoundly factor. How they're actualized may appear to be unique for various individuals, contingent upon a person's eating routine inclinations and objectives. The nourishments you eat as cheat dinners will likewise differ from individual to individual because of individual tastes, yet they frequently comprise of fatty nourishments that wouldn't generally be allowed on a common eating routine arrangement.

It's alright on the off chance that you extricate up on occasion and treat yourself to something you've been biting the dust for. There ought to be room in your eating routine for the intermittent guilty pleasure in any event when you are attempting to get in shape. There is no particular rule for when or how oftentimes your cheat dinner or day ought to happen. Regularly individuals will incorporate one cheat for each week, yet this can change contingent upon what the individual's wellbeing or weight reduction objectives are. Note that the cheat dinner approach isn't suitable for all eating routine styles. A few counts calories, for example, the vegetarian diet, require very severe adherence with no space for deceiving. In this way, the cheat procedure is best used in eats fewer carbs that take into consideration some adaptability. Weight the executives and body structure changes are perplexing procedures. Not every person will react a similar path to similar methodologies — the best diet plan is the one you can adhere to. It's notable that on the off chance that you eat less calories than you consume, weight reduction is probably going to happen. Thusly, the reward-based cheat feast or cheat day technique might be powerful in case you're ready to execute a well-arranged eating regimen and keep up in general decreased calorie consumption. It's much of the time guaranteed that utilizing cheat dinners will prompt quantifiable changes in body piece and improved metabolic capacity because of vacillations in the appetite hormone leptin. A typical weight the board hypothesis is that with lower levels of flowing leptin, you're bound to indulge in light of the fact that you need more of the hormone sending you flag that you're fulfilled and full. This may prompt bounce back weight gain.

A few people can viably oppose allurement, realizing that their cheat day is coming up, yet not every person can control their own eating practices similarly. Along these lines, similar outcomes can't be ensured for each individual. Fruitful and supported weight reduction is about more than eating less calories than you consume in a day. Your mentality toward nourishment can likewise altogether affect your capacity to oppose allurement and direct eating practices. Since the cheat feast or day technique centers on a reward-based framework, it might be ineffectual for the individuals who make some troublesome memories automatic passionate eating. A few people may even encounter sentiments of sadness and blame. Indeed, even a cheat dinner or day ought to be drawn closer refreshingly and with an arrangement. Tricking ought not to mean you disregard craving and satiety signs under the supposition that you can eat as much as you need of any nourishment on your cheat day. Similarly, as with any weight reduction or diet plan, it's significant that the cheat supper methodology is drawn closer with a solid attitude nearby practical objectives and desires that will bolster both mental and physical wellbeing. Numerous individuals who are hoping to have "non-vegetarian cheat days" or be "low maintenance veggie lover" are not simply pondering occasion suppers—

they're additionally considering when they're eating out at eateries or having at a companion's evening gathering. The main genuine issues with non-veggie lover cheat days are altogether founded on the moral standards of veganism. In this way, if your explanation behind being veggie lover is to improve your wellbeing for the most part, at that point the appropriate response is entirely clear: Yes, you can have non-vegetarian cheat days or cheat dinners. Cheat days are tied in with resetting digestion. In case you're on a caloric shortage, the "counter catabolic stage" of the eating regimen goes on for such a long time. After a while, the breakdown of fat, as well as muscle, starts. Spike days help counteract this while resetting digestion and craving hormones (leptin, ghrelin, and so forth.). There are additionally side advantages identified with absorption and giving your catalysts assortment.

A support and muscle-building diet, where the student eats in a caloric deficiency consistently, and afterward has a major cheat day. Individuals who are profound into "Super compensation Mode" may get pretty much spike days, from just a solitary week by week cheat supper, to week after week half-day cheats, week after week, entire day cheats, and entire day in addition to half-day swindles each week. The appeal of the cheat dinner is self-evident: you get the opportunity to eat stuff that is generally untouchable and incredibly flavorful. You get the opportunity to pull out all the stops for a night. It resembles excursion, and you're a nourishment traveler. Be that as it may, are there genuine advantages? The cheat supper is an incredible method to take the heap off, let free, and keep up your mental soundness. It can guarantee dietary consistency, and there's even late proof that it might make your eating regimen increasingly powerful The cheat feast resembles the reload week in quality preparing in that it helps the individuals who need it recharge their will to finish what has been started and consent to the eating regimen. It's a break from the repetitiveness, the passion, the difficult work — anything you desire to call it, and anyway you see it. Extended calorie limitation in the quest for weight reduction, regardless of whether conscious (gauging, estimating, tallying) or unconstrained (low-carb, center around supplement thickness to advance satiety), can discourage metabolic rate and slow down weight reduction. It is known. A cheat feast can kickstart the digestion and prop the weight reduction up, not regardless of the gigantic convergence of calories but since of it. At the point when you eat a major feast, a couple of beneficial things occur, Glycogen tops off. In case you're falling off a low-carb diet, a cheat supper brimming with carbs can restock your glycogen stores and make resulting high-power, anaerobically-requesting wellness interests progressively productive.

Leptin increments.

Leptin is a hormone that communicates with the nerve center to smother nourishment admission and increment vitality use. It's decreased by low degrees of muscle to fat ratio (muscle to fat ratio really secretes leptin) and delayed caloric limitation. So in the event that you've lost muscle to fat ratio before, slowed down, and further decreased nourishment admission to bust the level, you're doing a one-two punch on leptin.

Advantages of cheat dinners.

There is an unavoidable issue mark over the advantages of cheat suppers. Some contend that they ought to never be remembered for the eating routine since it is tied in with taking "terrible" calories. Others contend that periodic and particularly well-arranged deceiving can bring a few advantages. What are the realities about incorporating cheat dinners in your eating regimen?

They increment thyroid hormone generation

At the point when you are in a calorie deficiency, your body produces less T3 and T4 hormones. These are iodinated amino acids that manage quality articulation in the body by comparable components as steroid hormones. They are likewise basic for the thyroid organ to work appropriately. It is simply cheating dinners that are utilized to, in part, increment these hormones.

They are appropriate for competitors

During exercise, the polysaccharide glycogen, which is found in the liver and muscles, is discharged from the body. It is significant for controlling glucose levels and gives the muscles the essential vitality. The most straightforward approach to exhaust glycogen is through exercise. To expand glycogen levels in your muscles, you have to devour starches. In the event that you are struggling with excess weight that you have gained and you really need to cut it off, then a cheat dessert that is only allowed to be taken only once in a blue moon might actually come in very handy and greatly assist you in achieving your goal. In the event that you, at times think and even feel that it is a lot to do, this cheat meal will definitely work wonders for you as you continue with your vegetable eating diet throughout the time you had planned. In the event that you wind up hangover on the grounds that you attempted one of your companion's French fries the previous evening, a customary cheat supper may have the option to develop more strength. In any case, they aren't essential. The measure of time it takes to get again into that pined for fat-consuming zone will fluctuate dependent on the individual, yet it, for the most part, takes one to three days. Getting back in is likely extraordinary for every individual, and it relies upon the degree of carb limitation you decide to do. A few people do well with taking parts from a prohibitive eating routine, while others make some hard memories getting over into it. In the event that you are ending up expecting to take crushes or experiencing difficulty getting spirit into it. An issue with both transient preliminaries referenced on feast recurrence is that the enhanced gatherings had a bigger admission of both protein and absolute vitality than the non-enhanced gatherings. It can't be decided out that it is the extra enhanced protein/vitality and not the expanded feast recurrence that has caused an impact. Short term ponders just measure changes throughout the following hardly any hours in the wake of preparing, while protein amalgamation is raised for as long as 48 hours after a quality instructional course.

Cheat supper bodes well, particularly for the individuals who can stick to a very severe eating regimen plan and exercise hard in the rec center. They enjoy a little reprieve before coming back to a sound eating regimen. In this way, they are extremely famous with competitors and wellness lovers. At present, cheat dinners have an extraordinary effect on the treatment of maladies identified with gorging. Pigging out Disorder (BED) is a dangerous yet treatable illness described by intermittent scenes of eating a lot of nourishment. Along these lines, individuals experiencing this issue create mental issues, for example, sentiments of disgrace, dread or blame. One kind of treatment for dietary issues is the utilization of severe dietary consumes fewer calories. In such cases, cheat suppers are utilized to make it simpler for individuals to battle the malady. The incorporation of cheat suppers prompts a decrease in dietary problems in individuals with a propensity to nourishment reliance or powerlessness to control their dietary patterns. The inquiry regularly emerges whether it is smarter to cheat in your eating plan just with one dinner daily or to incorporate the supposed "cheat day" in the arrangement. That implies you can bear to eat anything you desire one entire day of the week. In any case, is it right to leave your regular feast plan for so long? It's about inspiration. The fundamental job of cheat dishes is to emphatically impact the mind of man. In some cases, it is extremely hard to keep up an exacting eating regimen and the possibility that, for instance, on Sunday, you can enjoy one cheat feast is an extraordinary inspiration. By devouring unhealthy suppers for the duration of the day, your exertion you have made so far might be squandered.

Rule 90/10.

Have you previously known about this standard? It essentially implies that 90% of the time, you ought to eat as indicated by your eating regimen plan, and 10% of the time, you can enjoy any enticement. Eating cheat dinner along these lines won't pulverize your wellness objectives.

Be that as it may, even a cheat supper ought not to be a greasy super calorie bomb. In the event that you have chosen to cheat, attempt to discover better options in contrast to mechanically handled nourishments.

CHAPTER 7:
A MONTH MEAL PLAN.

Is it true that you are keen on moving to a different vegetable only eating habit? Even if you hope to achieve and do away with the possibilities of illnesses such as diabetes and actually do something that is directly and positively impacting your life, starting with a vegetable-only diet can assist you achieve your goal. Do not worry, this booklet offers you with a whole month's guide on how to start with a plant-based meal for beginners, and it will walk you throughout the entire journey as you see some entire changes in your lifestyle. The term plant-based eating regimen or entire nourishment plant-based eating routine has been picking up in notoriety. Be that as it may, what do they really mean? Does it mean you never eat any creature items, similar to a vegetarian diet, or devour creature items with some restraint? There's a great deal of dispute about these terms. Numerous sources concur a plant-based diet is eating generally plant-based nourishment with practically zero creature items. In any case, a few sources would contend it is an eating routine of just plants, comparing it with a vegetarian diet.

A plant-based diet has, to a greater degree, an emphasis on eating entire, natural nourishments. Basically, here only a portion of the nourishments included:

- Soybeans and plants like legumes that have proteins.

- Milk and seeds.

- Fruits that contain healthy fats such as avocados.

- A lot of kales and spinach.

- Products of the soil, such as carrots.

- Naturally happening starches, similar to yams and sweet potatoes, Irish potatoes.

- Oats, rice, and whole grains.

- Coffee is incorporated.

Not at all like different sorts of diets, you can appreciate an assortment of nourishments, and you can even get yourself some dim chocolate! Since you realize what sorts of nourishments we're concentrating on, how about we investigate the dinner plans. Don't hesitate to blend and match – a portion of the snacks would be extraordinary for supper, and the other way around.

This plant-based eating routine dinner plan is directly for you in case you're hoping to eat more plants! The plans in this feast plan are simple veggie-lover plans. As noted above, don't hesitate to work in veggie lover or fish plans too dependent on how you'd like to describe plant-based. Squeezed paste: Place it in a little container that contains a half diced kabocha that is squeezed together with three butternuts. Later, pour in some milk close by one cup of freshwater. Allow them to cook until they are soft. Put the paste that you were able to make in a blender cup and add in some oil then later blend on a high speed to achieve a smoother paste. Make sure that you have enough water and oil to achieve this. Next, put in a little bit of pepper and salt in the previous container. Make sure that the salt and pepper to taste. For the squash and mushroom you will need the olive oil in a measuring container. This will form a caramel-like paste, and that is the point that you will add in some garlic and pour it in the container. Next, pour in the sauté squash as you gradually mix with olive oil to achieve a smooth paste. Add garlic to taste. This is the point as to which you will be required to mix up the two pastes with a touch of parsley and salt.

As for the rice, heat a little mix of the vegetables and allow them to simmer down in a little pot. In a bigger pot, pour in olive oil and a portion of the chopped onions and allow them to cook to a medium point where the onions will be more soft and goldish. Put the pre-boiled rice and continue cooking for averagely the next 6 minutes. Start to bit by bit incorporate vegetable stock a little on the double to empower the rice to totally hold liquid. Keep on progressively cook on medium warmth until liquid is finished. At the point when you are content with the delicacy of the rice, put in a protected spot, and keep warm.

When plating this food, make sure that the mushroom and squash puree and warm enough. Mixt it with the boiled rice as if seasoning. Incorporate portion of the squash/mushroom mix into rice and softly blend. Spot risotto in focal point of colossal plate, softly tap the base of the plate to empower rice to spread out. Spot staying besting over rice and sprinkle cut sage on top to wrap up.

Nutty spread and banana are only one of those can't-lose combos. It's a delicious, generous, and filling blend that makes a sweet treat that is likewise healthfully rich. Nutty spread is broadly high in protein. In the meantime, bananas are a known powerhouse of supplements, including high potassium and fiber levels. Together, these scrumptious fixings make a healthy, immediately empowering feast. This Peanut Butter Banana Overnight Oats formula is absolutely no special case.

With all the flavorful, invigorating medical advantages of nutty spread and bananas, this speedy and simple make-ahead breakfast formula will fulfill. It additionally helps its nourishing profile with almond milk and chia seeds. It's the ideal sweet and delicious, high-protein approach to begin your day.

Superfood avocado, as of now makes avocado toast a solid method to begin (or even end) the day. Stuffed with omega-3's, nutrient C, fiber, and bounty more nutrients and minerals, there's an explanation people go insane for this velvety green organic product. This white bean avocado toast kicks thing up a score, including a layer of crushed white beans underneath the velvety avocado spread. This packs in additional protein that will keep you feeling full and centered. Perhaps the best thing about avocado toast is the manner by which flexible it is. While the essentials are in the title, there are a lot of different approaches to dress it up. This triple-layer white bean avocado toast is finished off with new, cut cherry tomatoes. Spread on a cut of entire grain toast for a sound, flavorful breakfast or tidbit.

Also, these exquisite plans enhance the crushed white beans with gritty tahini and lively lemon. In the event that you've never attempted tahini, it's most likely going to be your new most loved thing. It's a center eastern spread produced using sesame seeds, and it has a rich, gritty flavor. Lemon and tahini truly add some additional something to this appetizing breakfast. It's not, in every case, simple to locate a solid breakfast that is additionally extraordinary to snatch and go. This white bean avocado toast is the entirety of the above mentioned. It might taste gourmet. However, you can get this basic formula ready in a short time or less.

Ingredients mix:

- Cayenne
- Black Pepper
- 2 Jalapeño
- 2 Mint
- ¼ Cilantro
- 3 Parsley
- Shallot
- 1 ground Cumin
- 1 ground Coriander
- 1 gram Chickpeas
- 3 ½ liters Water

- Salt

- 3 pcs Garlic

The cooking procedure.

Garlic and Tahini Sauce:

- 1 cup tahini

- 2 t Garlic

- 1 t Coriander

- Cumin

- ¼ C Water

Expel garlic required. Mix all the ingredients in a blender and blend so as to achieve a smooth paste. Use pepper and salt to season.

Hummus:

- Cayenne

- 1 Tahini

- chopped Garlic

- Cumin

- Lemon juice

- Coriander

- Cooked Chickpeas

Spot everything in a nourishment processor and heartbeat until smooth. On the off chance that the outcomes turn out excessively thick, don't hesitate to add fluid from peas to disperse. Use pepper and salt to season.

Baba Ghanoush:

- Lemon Juice

- 1 Za'taar

- 2 chopped Garlic

- Lemon Juice

- 1 ½ Cumin

- Coriander

- Cayenne

- Tahini

Put all the ingredients in a blender and blend them to achieve a smooth paste. Use pepper and salt to season.

Cucumber Tomato Salad:

- Tomatoes

- ½ t Mint

- Chickpeas

- 1 T Avocado

- Red Onion

- Za'taar Spice

- 1 Persian Cucumber

- 4 Basil Leaves

- Parsley

Combine all of them in a container leave it for around 29 minutes to settle before serving it. Use pepper and salt to season. at that point, decorate with basil leaves.

To plate: Arrange the two plunges and serving of mixed greens on a plate. Cut pita into quarters, at that point tenderly slice the falafel. Toast pita until marginally roasted.

Peach Pie Breakfast Parfait

This parfait overflows with all the sweetness you love from your preferred summer dessert. Luckily, our form fulfills those desires without fixing your entire day before it even starts. Made with coconut milk and chia seeds, this formula hits two wellbeing nourishment high notes. An ideal, supplement rich lactose substitute, coconut milk additionally supports enhance. In the meantime, superfood chia seeds pack huge amounts of fiber, minerals, and enemies of oxidants. They additionally happen to be an incredible option to the surface assortment of your parfait! Improved with maple syrup and enhanced with cinnamon, this parfait gets your three-day weekend to a normally sweet start. Obviously, peaches are actually the superstar here. Pressed with fiber, potassium, and nutrient C, this organic product is the ideal method to begin your day. Hurled in cinnamon, this tasty peach layer reviews your preferred pie filling. Also, with every single clean fixing, the organic product's regular flavor can truly sparkle. Topped with granola, this formula is sweet, light, and filling. It may not be peach pie grandmother's way; however, it is a righteous method to have dessert for breakfast.

Veggie lover Mango-Almond Milkshake

Mangoes are local to Asia and have gone far and wide because of their fame as delectable stone organic product. There are various assortments, changing in sweetness, flavor, and supplements however what they all share for all intents and purpose is the indisputable delectable flavor and key supplements of the organic product. Alongside a high vitality esteem, they are plentiful in dietary fiber and nutrient C. Mixing them into drinks is exceptionally normal in Asia.

Also, being basically a late spring natural product, they are best-appreciated virus.

Fixings

- 1 ready mango, mash
- 3/4 cup almond milk, unsweetened
- Ice

Directions

1. Put every one of the fixings in a blender and mix until smooth.

2. Drink right away.

Veggie lover Avocado Spinach Smoothie

Fixings

- 2 cups chilled almond milk
- Ice
- 1 avocado
- 2 tablespoons Agave nectar
- 1/2 cup spinach

Guidelines

1. Blend, join every one of the fixings and heartbeat until smooth.

2. Serve cold.

Chocolate Chip Banana Pancakes

The formula calls for essentially no milk items. Rather, this formula chooses sound, veggie lover amicable fixings like coconut oil and coconut milk. Most flapjacks call for margarine or vegetable oil, yet swapping these traditional elements for coconut oil does the dish an entire bundle of wellbeing related favors. Coconut oil positions high on our rundown of mind-boggling superfoods. It brings down your awful cholesterol, advances heart wellbeing, and brings down your danger of coronary illness.

Then, you don't need to suffocate these cakes with maple syrup. Velvety bananas and coconut sugar normally improve the hotcakes, saving you the boatload of sugar and void calories you get from syrup. Bananas give these yummy cakes a significant flavor support while conveying a lot of nutrients and minerals like potassium, calcium, manganese, magnesium, iron, and B6. Nature's vitality sponsor, bananas convey the fuel you have to vanquish the day. The healthful powerhouse keeps your glucose unfaltering, your mind alert, and your digestion running solid!

Lastly, we've picked entire wheat flour rather than white flour, kicking the formula's dietary benefit up a couple of indents with its complex carbs and fiber.

Fixings

- Veggie lover chocolate chips,

- coconut oil,

- Wheat flour

- Coconut milk

- 1 huge excessively ready banana, crushed 1 1/2 cups entire wheat flour

- 1 teaspoon preparing pop

- Chips 2 tablespoons coconut sugar

Directions

1. In a huge blending bowl, consolidate the banana, sugar, oil, and milk. Blend well to join. Include the flour and heating pop, cautiously mix until simply joined. Be mindful so as not to over blend. Tenderly overlap in the chocolate chips.

2. Lightly splash a skillet with non-stick shower and warmth on medium heat. Pour around 1/4 cup of the hitter into the skillet. Cook around 5 minutes, or until flapjacks start to rise in the middle. Cautiously flip and cook for another 2 to 3 minutes. When cooked, expel flapjack from the container and rehash the procedure until all the player has been utilized. Oil the skillet as required with non-stick splash in the middle of cooking the flapjacks.

3. Serve hot, whenever wanted top with maple syrup, nectar, coconut spread, crisp natural product, or your preferred jam!

Fiery Kale Salad with Chickpeas and Maple Dijon Dressing

Extremely, there's nothing not to adore about this serving of mixed greens. The chickpeas get a flavor support by means of zesty cayenne and stew pieces, which consolidates flawlessly with the fiery jalapenos in the serving of mixed greens. The carrots and red onion give a sweet, crunchy enhance. And afterward, there's the nutritious kale – wearing a maple Dijon dressing, you won't see any of those normally severe flavors.

These beans are definitely not typical beans. Not at all like different sorts of vegetables, chickpeas (otherwise called garbanzo beans) keep up their structure truly well. They have a rich surface and a nutty flavor with a marginally grainy, chewy outside. They're an ideal balance to super crunchy fixings like kale, carrots, and carrots.

Fixings

Salad:

- jalapeno pepper,

- 3 cups kale, generally cleaved

- 1/2 cup red onion, cut into slender strips

- 1/4 teaspoon red pepper pieces

- 1 (15 ounce) can chickpeas, depleted and washed

- 1/2 cup carrot, destroyed

- Cayenne pepper

For the Dressing:

- apple juice vinegar

- maple syrup

- 1 teaspoon orange get-up-and-go

- Dijon mustard

Directions

For Salad:

1. In a medium bowl, consolidate the chickpeas, cayenne pepper, and red pepper pieces. Hurl well to cover the chickpeas in the flavors.

2. In a huge bowl, consolidate the chickpeas and the rest of the serving of mixed greens fixings. Prepare well to join and place the blended plate of mixed greens into serving bowls. Sprinkle with around 3 teaspoons of dressing and serve.

For the Dressing:

1. Combine all fixings and whisk well. Let sit for 5 minutes. Give the dressing a fast mix before showering over the plate of mixed greens.

Avocado Hummus Bowl.

A strengthening blend of veggies and hummus to top you off with supplements. It's the ideal evening lift me up when you feel a vitality crash going ahead.

Chickpeas contain solid portions of fiber, protein, and iron, basic for fortress. Cucumbers, cherry tomatoes, carrots, and spinach consolidated contain a huge amount of nutrients and minerals with a low-glycemic record to keep your glucose levels stable for the duration of the day.

This dish is incredibly simple to plan.

Fixings

- 1/2 ready avocado, stripped, set, and thickly cut
- 1/2 cup chickpeas (from a 15-ounce can), depleted and flushed
- 1/2 medium measured cucumber, meagerly cut
- 2/3 cup grape or cherry tomatoes
- 1 cup child carrots
- 10 spinach leaves, well-cleaned
- 1/3 cup clean eating hummus, any assortment, locally acquired or custom made
- 2 tablespoons pumpkin or shelled sunflower seeds, discretionary
- A teaspoon legitimate or ocean salt
- 1/4 teaspoon dark pepper

Directions

1. Line a bowl with spinach leaves, layering if fundamental.

2. Add avocado cuts to one corner, chickpeas to another, grape tomatoes to another, and child carrots to another.

3. Add hummus to the middle and top with sunflower or pumpkin seeds, if utilizing.

4. Sprinkle the entire dish with salt and pepper and appreciate!

5. This is incredible for a to-go lunch when made in a versatile compartment with a top.

Butternut Squash and Cranberry Quinoa Salad.

Everybody that gets to taste it always ends up cherishing its remarkably nutty, sweet, rich flavor. It is ideal to use in soups, goulashes, bread, or cooked with flavors.

This plate of mixed greens is chocked-loaded with nutrients and minerals. The superfood quinoa contributes heart-solid monounsaturated fat, omega-3 unsaturated fat, manganese, Vitamin E, and numerous different supplements. The butternut squash includes fiber, Vitamin C, manganese, magnesium, and potassium. This amazing combo makes for a staggeringly supplement rich dish.

Fixings

- 1/3 cup pecans

- 5 tablespoons of olive oil

- A teaspoon of dark pepper

- 1/2 cup dried cranberries

- 3 cups butternut squash, diced little

- 1 tablespoon slashed basil

- 1/4 teaspoon ocean salt

- 2 cups cooked quinoa

Headings

1. Put 3 big spoons of the oil in a container that is just medium in size. Cook it in low heat until it is smooth and tender.

2. Using a small bowl, mix all the other ingredients that include: cranberries, walnuts, pepper, squash, quinoa by adding 2 big tablespoons of the olive oil.

Apple and Fresh Thyme with Butternut Squash Soup.

There is nothing better than a very warm or liberal soup in the cool winter months when it gets very cold at times! With winter squash at its zenith, Butternut Squash Soup with Apple and Fresh Thyme is an unprecedented technique to hold a segment of fall's best flavors. Kids and adults, the equivalent, will venerate the normal sweetness of the butternut squash and apples, and the new thyme incorporates just enough pizzazz. Soups with the two apples and new thyme may sound fairly sporadic, yet when these fixings get together, they make the squash taste all the better!

Fixings

- 24 ounces chicken stock
- low-fat milk
- Butternut squash, diced 2 cups
- 1 Granny Smith Apple diced
- Red onion
- Garlic
- Salt and pepper to taste
- ¼ cumin
- Olive oil
- Thyme leaves

Steps:

1. use a large container and heat the olive oil on a low, medium heat. Include the onion and garlic and sauté until

fragrant. Include the squash and apple and mix to cover them in oil.

2. Cover and lessen the warmth. Enable the vegetables to perspire for 5-7 minutes. Check occasionally to ensure the vegetables aren't caramelizing.

3. Add the stock, thyme, and cumin. Stew for 20 minutes or until the veggies are delicate.

4. Add drain and puree in a blender. Serve warm.

Combination Lunch Burritos

We've all had Asian spring rolls. Without plunging sauce, eatery style spring rolls totally need enhance. To make them satisfactory, they are normally presented with a nut or soy sauce. In any case, consider it, aren't spring rolls fundamentally combination lunch burritos – a serving of mixed greens moved up in a rice wrapper? Indeed, and no. Solidified and café spring rolls are pan-fried and oily, making them not all that sound lunch.

This combination lunch burritos formula will change the manner in which you take a gander at lunch! A serving of three of these will fulfill your stomach and leave you liking having a super scrumptiously sound supper. They check in at under 200 calories and are loaded up with vitality advancing fixings.

Don't hesitate to switch up the vegetables in the filling, however, attempt to pick a vegetable of each shading to expand your wholesome admission. What's more, as usual, drop us a line in the remarks and let us know how it went. We couldn't want anything more than to catch wind of your fun, imaginative interpretation of these combination lunch burritos!

Fixings

- 18 rice paper wrappers
- 8 ounces dark colored rice noodles, prescribe Annie Chun's Maifun Brown Rice Noodles
- 5 ounces blended child greens, natural if conceivable
- 1 avocado
- 1 cucumber
- 2 chime peppers, your decision of shading
- 2 cups of destroyed carrots
- 2 cups destroyed purple cabbage
- 1 (16 ounce) bundle firm or too Firm Square of tofu

Veggie lover without oil serving of mixed greens dressing – your decision

Guidelines

1. Prepare the rice noodles as indicated by bundle directions and afterward channel.

2. Peel and cut the avocado, cucumber, and the chime peppers into matchstick width strips.

3. Prepare the tofu boards as portrayed in this formula, without the marinade, and afterward cut it into matchstick width strips.

4. Add the vegetable fillings to a huge bowl; at that point, prepare and cover generously with the vegetarian without oil serving of mixed greens dressing of your decision.

5. Prepare the rolls exclusively by submerging each sheet of rice wrapper in turn in a bowl of warm water for about 10 seconds, at that point place on a cutting board or other clean level work surface.

6. Layer an even measure of plate of mixed greens filling crosswise over lower third of rice wrapper, leaving room on sides to fold edges for your burrito spring rolls.

7. Layer an even measure of tofu strips and rice noodles over plate of mixed greens filling, at that point overlay over edge folds and fold your burritos into completely encased cylinders.

8. The fixings recorded should make around 18 completed rolls. Spot completed moves on a serving plate, and be certain not to stack them, as they will stay together.

9. Eat, grin, and feel sound!

Antiquated Potato Salad | Plant-Based Recipes

Antiquated potato plate of mixed greens is one of my preferred side dishes. It's rich and smooth, loaded up with fulfilling flavors that supplement various distinctive principle dishes. You can serve it up during an easygoing patio grill simply with respect to a fancier, plunk down evening gathering. What's more, it surely doesn't hurt that it's anything but difficult to make and doesn't break the calorie bank, either! The main issue with great potato plate of mixed greens plans is such mayonnaise.

This formula couldn't be simpler to make, either. Just hurl all the mayonnaise fixings into a powerful blender and heartbeat until everything has a rich consistency. You can even thin it out with water in the event that you lean toward a more slender mayonnaise for an all the more softly covered potato plate of mixed greens.

At the point when everything meets up, we figure you may like this Plant-Based, Old-Fashioned Potato Salad Recipe superior to the first formula. Its evidence that veggie lover cooking can be full-enhanced and completely delightful.

Fixings

- 2 pounds of red potatoes, with skins

- 1 tablespoon of genuine or ocean salt

- 1/2 paprika (for decorate), discretionary

Plant-Based Mayonnaise

- 1 cup crude cashews + 2 cups water for splashing

- Cleaved dill weed

- Water

- White wine vinegar

- Garlic powder

- Lemon juice

Directions

1. Rinse and scour potatoes, cut into 3D shapes, around 1-1/2 inches. Include potatoes and 1 tablespoon salt to an

enormous pot, totally spread potatoes with water and heat to the point of boiling. Lessen warmth to a low-bubble. Cook until potatoes are delicate when penetrated with a fork, 15-20 minutes. Channel potatoes cover and put in a safe spot.

2. While potatoes are cooking, add cashews to a huge bowl, spread with 2 cups water, and permit to set 15 minutes. Deplete and flush cashews.

3. Add flushed cashews and 3/4 cup water to a blender, beat until a rich consistency. Empty blend into a blending bowl.

4. Add outstanding fixings, with the exception of red onions and celery, to the cashew/water blend. Speed until very much joined. Note: mayo will thicken up following a few hours, and is best when made the prior night.

5. Add onions and celery to potatoes, hurl to consolidate.

6. Pour around 1 cup of mayo over the potatoes, hurl to consolidate. Include extra mayo for a definitive velvety potato plate of mixed greens. Include extra salt whenever the need arises. Gently sprinkle the top with some paprika.

7. Cover and refrigerate it for about 2 to 3 hours before serving it when it is still cool.

Quinoa Lentil Burger

Our quinoa lentil burger recipe is stacked with improve, anyway contains high proportions of supplements and minerals to help thwart dangerous development and lower cholesterol. Quinoa lentil burgers make sure to satisfy your wants for a burger with decidedly no fault. Each burger has 13 grams of fiber, 17 grams of protein, and only 9 grams of fat. To the degree sound burgers go, this one is tops!

With gigantic measures of flavors and nectar Dijon mustard to add to the delicious taste, quinoa lentil burgers are magnificent when cooked on the fire sear and beat with a lovely thick cut of fresh tomato and a leaf or two of lettuce

Fixings

Burger Recipe:

- Pepper and salt
- Garlic powder
- Red onion
- 1 can of diced green chilies

- 1 cup of whole-wheat panko bread pieces

- cooked quinoa

- 2 teaspoons of olive oil

- Oats

- White Whole Wheat Flour

- Cornstarch

- Cumin powder

- 1 teaspoon of paprika

- 1 cup cooked lentils

Nectar Dijon Mustard Recipe

- 1 and a half tablespoons Dijon Mustard

- 2 teaspoons nectar

Rules

1. Thoroughly join all burger fixings in a large container, create portions that resemble 4 burgers sizes. In tremendous skills, on medium warmth, add 1 tablespoon olive oil, remember to cook until darker for the different sides, around 10-12 minutes. Acknowledge with your favored bun or move, spread on Honey Dijon Mustard at whatever point needed

2. Make the Dijon mustard by joining the fixings and allowing to refrigerate it until the moment of serving.

3. Sauté onion in 2 teaspoons olive oil until sensitive, around 4 minutes.

4. Suggested fixings: sautéed mushrooms, tomato, red onion, romaine lettuce, and Honey Dijon Mustard

The most effective method to Make Spicy Mango Salsa

Salsas are an incredible method to add virtuous flavor to your preferred dinner. Most importantly, it adds an explosion of shading to your feast. We as a whole, realize that we eat with our eyes, so simply reveal to me that you wouldn't have any desire to eat up this wonderful-looking fiery mango salsa! Furthermore, it packs in an insane measure of flavor. The mix of sweet and zesty will truly add a pleasant profundity to a basic fish and rice supper or hurl it on tortillas, and you'll have the best fish tacos. It's solid! Serve it up with a side of chips or thud it on a bed of greens and consider it a plate of mixed greens. Regardless of what you do with this solid salsa, it'll taste extraordinary. It's normally low in fat and calories, with next to no carb-forward fixings. What's more, this hot mango salsa is totally sans gluten and without dairy

Fixings

- 1 medium mango, stripped, pit evacuated and diced little

- 6 Roma tomatoes, diced little

- 1 little red onion, diced little

- 1 little red chime pepper, diced little

- 1 jalapeno,

Guidelines

1. In an enormous bowl, join the mango, tomato, onion, pepper, and jalapeno, blend will. Mix in the rest of the fixings. Tenderly hurl just to join.

2. Let sit for 15 minutes before serving. Present with tortilla or pita chips as an afterthought. Incredible over fish tacos

Veggie lover Spinach and Artichoke Dip

This is an incredible formula for when you want to nibble on some plunge yet do not need all the extra included calories and added substances. It utilizes just the regular fixings and is certainly more beneficial than its dairy-filled partner. The extraordinary thing about this formula is that it genuinely doesn't lose the flavor in any event when "vegetarian sizing" it.

Fixings

- 4 garlic

- 1 bundle solidified hacked spinach

- 1 low-fat smooth tofu

- Lemon juice

- 1 onion

- 1 quartered artichoke

Guidelines

1. Heat 350 degrees C.

2. Put onion and garlic in an aluminum foil. Heat for 20 to 30 minutes.

3. Place the spinach in drying towel. Crush and curve the drying towel to press out however much water as could be expected to come from the spinach.

4. Place all the ingredients in a nourishment processor or Blend and heartbeat until all-around cleaved. Include the

rest of the fixings and procedure until just marginally thick or smooth – your inclination.

5. Serve with newly heated tortilla chips, wafers, or crisp cut veggies.

Chocolate Peanut Butter Energy Bites

Two delicious treats star in this formula for partition controlled scaled-down balls. These nourishments brag a low-glycemic record, adding to sentiments of totality and a steady arrival of vitality that goes on for a considerable length of time. Pop one of these vitality nibbles to keep away from an evening crash and fulfill your sweet tooth.

Fixings

- Red Peppers
- Half a cup flax seeds
- 1 cup of normal rich nutty spread,
- 3 chia seeds
- 1 teaspoon of salt
- 1 cup of cocoa powder, crude
- A half-cup of nectar or maple syrup
- 2 cups of antiquated moved oats, separated

■ 1 teaspoon genuine vanilla concentrate

Directions

1. Keep in the ice chest for a period of about 4 to 5 days or stop for as long as about fourteen days.

2. Put all the flax seeds and ground oats in a fairly huge bowl. Include the remaining cup of cocoa, chia seeds, salt, and oats. Blend the mixture so as to mix well.

3. Let it settle for a while.

4. Using a grinder, grind oats that are half a cup full together with the chia seeds until they are in powder form.

5. In a different little bowl, mix together the nectar, vanilla, and nutty spread separate until consolidated. Add to the enormous bowl of dry fixings and mix well to consolidate. Hands might be utilized to join as blend is thick. Put the portions in a measurement of an inch meatballs. This will enable you to make approximately 18 balls. Note that the balls will be perfect when the hand is wet with water, and by covering them in coconut oil shields the blend from adhering to hands while shaping the balls.

6. Note that if batter is excessively clingy, crush extra oats and include. On the off chance that mixture is excessively dry, include a touch progressively nutty spread.

Occasion Peppermint Fudge.

This peppermint fudge formula consolidates smooth, rich chocolate with the splendid taste of peppermint for a heavenly occasion treat. While huge amounts of fudge aren't suggested, in the event that you love the flavor of chocolate, denying all guilty pleasures can prompt inclination hopeless and even a gorge. Your most logical option is to eat little bits of your preferred nourishments and make them without any preparation, so you control the entirety of the fixings in each dish. Tasty pastries are an alternative when eating healthy, as long as you attempt to snack littler bits of treats made with clean fixings. Notwithstanding being extra yummy, chocolate can likewise be solid. It contains cancer prevention agents, so by reveling a bit, you are helping your body ensure itself and fend off poisons and remote trespassers.

Fixings

- 2 1/2 cups chocolate chips (for the medical advantages we utilize mixed dim chocolate chips)

- 1/3 cup canned (not the container coconut milk...canned is best for this formula)

- Palm sugar

- blended margarine (discretionary coconut oil)

- Dash of genuine or ocean salt

- 1 teaspoon unadulterated peppermint remove, discretionary vanilla concentrate

- 1/2 cup diced pecans (discretionary)

Directions

1. Add to an overwhelming pot chocolate chips, coconut milk, coconut sugar, margarine or coconut oil, and salt, mix to join. Go to low warmth and enable chocolate to totally dissolve, mix to counteract searing.

2. After chocolate has totally liquefied expel from heat, add peppermint and mix to consolidate. In the case of utilizing pecans, include, and mix.

3. Cool revealed until fudge is at room temperature.

4. Oil a 1-quart goulash dish. Empty into dish, refrigerate 4 hours or until firm. Cut to 30 squares.

CHAPTER 8:
PLANT-BASED RECIPES

Probably the ideal approaches to eating well is to (every so often) avoiding meat and going high on eating a lot of vegetables and go low maintenance plant-based. To kick you off, we have arranged out each meatless Monday for a period of a whole year. Presently you can concentrate on getting a charge out of occasional produce, kindness of brilliant servings of mixed greens and smooth pasta, rather than pondering, "What's for supper?" And in the event that you need to make arranging these dinners considerably simpler, you can plan every one of them into week by week menus utilizing your Cooking Light Diet membership.

Red Beans and Rice

Fixings:

Green beans.

- Hot Sauce
- Diced Carrots
- Bell Peppers
- 2 Red Onions

- Celery

- Dried Thyme

- Smoked Paprika

- Cayenne pepper

- Bay Leaf

- Dried Oregano

- Cumin powder

- Dried Red Beans

Mix all the ingredients in a large pot and add two glasses of water to the beans. Cook the stew on low, medium heat for a period of about 25 minutes. Mix every once in a while for a span of 40 minutes to an hour. When they become soft, use pepper and salt to season.

Rice

- Smashed Lemongrass

- Cilantro Leaves

- Kosher Salt

- Jasmine Brown Rice

Place all the ingredients into a rice cooker pot and allow the use of low heat until the rice is fully cooked. Add the red beans together with the cilantro leaves to the rice.

Toasted Coconut and Pineapple Oatmeal

Fixings:

- Cut Irish Oats

- Sea Salt

- 2 cups of Water

- Cup of sliced Pineapple

- Sliced Banana

- ½ Blueberries

- Toasted Shredded Coconut

- Coconut Milk

Toast destroyed coconut in little sauté dish until brilliant dark colored and put in a safe spot. Warm water, coconut milk, and ocean salt in a little container and allow to simmer. When bubbling, add oats and cook on low heat for about 20 to 25 minutes, blending sometimes. When oats are cooked to wanted surface, include half of all the foods grown from the ground coconut, at that point overlay together. Spot hot oats in medium bowl and embellishment with residual leafy foods.

Vegetable Chili and Vegan Corn Bread.

Stew:

- Bell Pepper
- Yellow Onion
- Carrots (Diced)
- Garlic
- Celery
- 2 Jalapeños
- Zucchini
- Yellow Squash
- Green Beans
- Kidney Beans
- Mushrooms
- Fire Roasted Tomatoes
- Vegetable Broth
- Bay Leaf
- Tomato Paste

- Olive Oil

- Thyme

- Chili Powder

- Basil

- Chipotle Powder

- Ground Cumin

- Oregano

- Rosemary

- 3 Basil Leaves

Heat the olive oil in a small container and put in the onions and allow them to simmer on low, medium heat until the onions change the color to golden brown. Then add the mushrooms celery and carrots then cook until they become soft. Later add the other important ingredients that include: squash, green beans, zucchini, and peppers, squash, and continue cooking for about 4 minutes on medium-low heat. Add the chilies and the garlic and cook until they mix together. Put in the dry ingredients and let them cook for 3 minutes. Next, include tomato paste and cook for 3 to 4 minutes. As you finish up, add the tomatoes, beans, and juices; make it form a stew and lower to medium heat. Cook for about 30 minutes; you can now season with salt and pepper. Put 3 cups of bean stew in a rapid blender and blend it until it becomes smooth, then add back to the pot, then mix it all together. Taste in order to check for the flavor once more, you can now place the stew in a medium bowl and top it all with basil and parsley.

Cornbread:

- Heating Powder
- Frozen Corn
- Warm Almond Milk
- Vanilla Extract
- Vegetarian Butter
- Yellow Cornmeal
- Fine Sea Salt
- Canned Roasted Jalapeno
- Heating Soda
- All-Purpose Flour
- Almond Milk
- Apple Cider Vinegar
- Flax Seed Powder

Heat the boiler to 400°F. Mix together the two warm flax seed and almond milk in a little container. Dissolve the margarine and let it stay warm. Mix them up together with the flour, cornmeal, and preparing the powder, heating pop, and salt in a little container. Using a different container bowl, mix the second measure of almond milk, apple juice vinegar, and vanilla, at that point add in the flaxseed blend until broken down. Pour the wet mixture over the dry mixture, at that point whisk just until they are evenly mixed; mix in the liquefied margarine. At that point, overlap in the diced jalapeño and defrosted corn. Move them into a gently lubed cast iron container and spread equally to all the edges. Heat the cornbread for at least 20 minutes. Cool it down completely before cutting it. Seal it completely at room temperature.

Veggie Enchiladas and Roasted Tomatillo Sauce

Cooked Tomatillo Sauce:

- Tomatillos

- Smoked Paprika

- Yellow Onions

- Garlic

- Cilantro Leaves

- Cayenne

- Fresh Lime Juice

- Chili Peppers

- Cumin

Dice the Tomatillos in the middle and dish skin side up in a 425-degree boiler for about 15 minutes or until it is roasted. Allow the tomatillos to cool, and dispose of any fluid that may be present. Put them all in a nourishment processor and heat until somewhat smooth. Finally, include the pepper and the salt.

Enchiladas:

- Olive Oil

- Roasted Tomatillo Sauce

- Zucchini

- Avocado

- Cauliflower

- Kidney Beans

- Poblano Pepper

- Yellow Onion

- White Corn

- Tomatoes

- Cilantro Leaves

- Cumin

- Corn Tortillas

- Cayenne

- Coriander

- Chili Powder

In a very large metallic container, put in the oil at medium heat and at that point, add in the onions. Gradually mix until they turn brownish. Next, add in the mushrooms and continue cooking, as you add in the zucchini, corn, and cauliflower. Cook until delicate. Now, add in every single dry ingredient until the fluid from the tomato is almost all gone. Then add in the 2 tb tomatillo sauce alongside 1 tb cilantro leaves; set it all aside to cool for a short while. Put a small amount of sauce in a little solid metal container or stove safe dish container. Add and fill the toasted tortillas with a veggie blend and roll. Put the enchiladas in container and spoon sauce over both, orchestrating simmered poblano pepper cuts over every one of the enchilada. Spread with thwart and prepare them for 15 minutes at 315 degrees.

Remove them from the stove; at that point garnish them with some more sauce and cilantro leaves.

Corn Spaghetti and Beyond "Meatballs":

- Garlic
- Black Pepper
- Dried Basil
- Dried Corn Spaghetti
- Beyond Meat
- Dried Oregano
- Cayenne
- Basil Leaves
- Tomato Sauce
- Chopped Parsley
- Dried Thyme

Put all the meat in a bowl and then add in every one of the dried ingredients and pepper, start molding them into small balls. Heat the mixture in a small container with the 'meatballs' and keep it constant at that warm temperature. Boil corn the pasta for ten to twelve minutes, squeeze, and add in some tomato sauce. Put in the meat and sauce in and around the pasta. Garnishing it with the parsley, basil, and crisp dark pepper.

Tomato Sauce:

- Canned Tomatoes

- Roma Tomatoes

- Tomato Paste

- Thyme

- Cayenne Pepper

- Bay Leaves

- Basil

- Bulb Garlic

- Oregano

- Tomato Juice

Remove the simmered garlic from their bulbs by first slowly removing the back skin and leaving boiled garlic cloves.

In a very large stock pot, mix all the ingredients together and cook on medium to low heat for about 35-45 minutes. When all the fluid is finished, then remove from the heat source and season it all with some pepper and salt. You can also put some sauce through a ricer or nourishment processor. In the case of properly using the nourishment processor, just heat the sauce for a while, but don't puree. Remove and add in the chili and herbs.

Nursery Vegetable Fajitas.

- Cilantro Leaves
- Red Pepper
- Portobello Mushrooms
- Corn Tortillas
- Caramelized Onions
- Garlic
- Zucchini Sliced

Heat the iron dish that you plan to use thoroughly for about 6 minutes until it is red hot. Put in all the vegetables and prepare for a minute, then put in the garlic, mix it all and then serve! Top it all with Cilantro Leaves

Prepared maize Tortillas:

Corn Tortillas

Season with cayenne, salt, cumin, and pepper. Prepare it at 395 degrees for about 10-15 minutes, remove it from the heat source and then sprinkle it with lime juice. Put in a safe, dry secure place.

Pico de Gallo:

- Lime Juice
- Red Onion
- Cayenne
- Tomato
- Cilantro Leaves
- Cumin
- Red Plum
- Lemon Juice
- Jalapeño with seeds

Put all the ingredients in a container, use salt and pepper to season and serve.

Bean stew Roasted Pineapple:

Pineapple

Season the pineapple with chipotle powder, salt, cumin, coriander, and pepper. Barbecue them on high heat source till they get fully burnt. Let it cool down then cut them.

Cooked Heirloom Pepper Soup and Vegetable Bruschetta.

Soup:

- Olive Oil
- Jalapeño
- Curry Powder
- Celery
- Bell Peppers
- Tomato
- Coriander
- Vegetable Stock
- Almond or Soy Milk
- Carrot
- Garlic
- Parsley
- Cilantro Leaves
- Onion

- Cayenne

- Cumin

- Basil Leaves

In a very big container, heat olive oil that measures one tablespoon on some medium heat. Put in the container onions and allow them to simmer until they change their color to a golden brown one. After doing so, add celery and carrot and allow them to cook until they are soft. Later you can simmer the mixture and put in the garlic for a period of 4 minutes. Reduce the heat as you put in the dry ingredients such as cayenne, coriander and curry powder. For a period of four minutes, nicely mix all the ingredients to ensure that they are well mixed. Put in the chopped tomatoes and allow them to cook until they are in liquid form. Put in the almonds and vegetables and prepare for about half an hour on little heat. Use salt and pepper while seasoning. Put in some limited quantities of the stew in a rapid blender and blend until smooth; cool it with ice.

Soup Garnish:

- Cherry Tomatoes

- Bell Pepper

- Mixed Mushrooms

- Onion

- Potatoes

Boil the potatoes in a container with salty water until they soften. Take the potatoes out of the container and let them cool off for a few minutes. Later, cut the potatoes down the middle, then prepare them in a little olive oil till they turn dark, this should only take around 3 to 5 minutes.

Now put the mushrooms in a little olive oil till they turn brownish, now add in some simmered pepper, tomatoes, and diced onions. Cook on medium heat until the tomatoes become soft and squashed. Now add in the cooked potatoes and the parsley.

Vegetable Bruschetta:

- Avocado

- Cherry Tomatoes

- Parsley

- Garlic

- Cucumber

- Seeded Bread

- Roasted Peppers

- Basil Leaves

Toast the bread, and then crush the garlic clove and smear it on the bread just before you start toasting. Mix all vegetables flavoring with pepper and salt. Then add the basil and parsley on top.

Vegetable Lo Mein Noodles.

Noodle Sauce:

- Sriracha Sauce

- Coconut Sugar

- Mushroom Soy Sauce

- Dark Soy Sauce

- Sesame Oil

- Light Soy Sauce

Blend all the ingredients in a small container and put it in a cool, dry, and secure place.

Lo Mein:

- Basil Leaves

- Spears Blanched and Asparagus

- Blanched Broccoli

- Egg Free Lo Mein Noodles

- Green Onions

- Carrots Julienne

- Red Onions

- Spinach

- Mushrooms

- Ginger

- Canola Oil

- Cilantro Leaves

- Noodle Sauce

- Garlic

In a large non-stick container, heat the oil on high heat. Add in the mushroom, onion, and carrots and cook till they soften. Add the garlic and lo aura noodles then cook them for about 2 to 3 minutes. Now add in the spinach, asparagus, broccoli, and ginger. Finally add in the noodle sauce then cook it for about 1 minute. Put in medium bowl and top it with herbs.

New Vegetable Tartine.

Fixings:

- Pumpkin Seeds

- Parsley

- French Radish

- Ripe Tomato

- Peppers

- Basil Leaves

- Seeded Bread

- Sunflower Seeds

- Blanched Asparagus

Season all the vegetables with pepper and salt to taste. Start with cut tomatoes, then the asparagus, boiled peppers, and the radish. Finally, finish with the toasted seeds and then the herbs.

Split Pea Soup with Pear and Mushroom Bruschetta.

Soup:

- Celery

- Onions

- Vegetable Stock

- Thyme

- Parsley

- Split peas

- Bay Leaves

- Fingerling Potatoes

- Cayenne

- Olive Oil

- Liquid Smoke

- Turmeric

- Carrots

- Garlic

- Lemon Juice

- Asparagus

In a large container, add in the garlic and onions until they are golden brown. Add in the celery and carrots then keep on cooking on medium heat until they soften. Now add in the dried flavors and splashed peas and cook until the flavors mix evenly. Add in the vegetable stock, fluid smoke and crisp thyme then cook on medium heat for about 20-30 minutes or until split peas are soft enough. Mix 2 cups of hot soup in a blender and blend them together till they become smooth and add back to the soup. Season soup with lemon juice, pepper, and salt to taste. Add potatoes and asparagus to the soup and serve in a medium container and top it with parsley.

Pear and Mushroom Bruschetta:

- Baguette

- Pear

- Mushrooms

- Parsley

Season the pears and the mushrooms with parsley, pepper, and salt to taste. Add the mushrooms to the toast, then put in the simmered pears over the mushrooms. Top it with parsley.

CHAPTER 9:
CHALLENGES OF A PLANT-BASED MEAL AND HOW TO BEAT THEM

As innumerable hopeful vegetarians are finding, the change from omnivore to herbivore is loaded with physical, social, and monetary difficulties — at any rate, for the individuals who don't have an individual culinary expert. The battle to surrender most loved nourishments like cheddar and margarine can be made all the harder by cruel words and eye-moving from unsympathetic loved ones. Substitutes like almond drain and rice milk can stun the taste buds, and veggie lover strength and accommodation nourishments can cost a few times what their meat and dairy counterparts do. What's more, new vegetarians rapidly find that numerous nourishments in supermarkets and on café menus have shrouded creature fixings.

B12

This is the thing that everybody appears to be worried about, in light of the fact that meats appear to be the main wellspring of the nutrient. It's numerous a meat-eaters pardon not to try and attempt; I additionally utilized it numerous a period. Be that as it may, for what reason is it so essential? It makes red platelets, in addition to other things.

There are a few evident side effects, including tiredness, discombobulating, and brevity of breath (as indicated by Google), in the event that you don't get enough of it.

Goals: Fear not, trying vegetarian, there are a lot of spots you can discover it. By and by, I wasn't too flustered in light of the fact that a month of not eating meat wouldn't cripple my B12 levels drastically, as my PCP companion let me know.

Baffling, as well, in the absence of social support. New vegetarians state it's difficult to surrender most loved nourishments and change in accordance with the flavor of substitutes for margarine and dairy items. Surrendering most loved nourishments is rarely simple, nourishment researcher's state, for it implies superseding taste inclinations engraved on the mind during a lifetime of eating. Veggie lover fixings and cooking strategies can be overpowering for novices, regardless of whether the progressions are moderately little. Substitutes like veggie-lover margarine and healthful yeast can give a not used to nutty or gooey flavor. Another technique for making vegetarian nourishments velvety or mushy includes splashing and mixing cashews.

Shopping for food

This vulnerability of whether a specific thing is veggie lover proceeds with while going shopping for food. I have consistently been very great at perusing marks in light of the fact that even as a veggie-lover, I needed to comprehend what I was eating, yet being vegetarian makes shopping for food considerably progressively troublesome as there are some extremely peculiar manners by which creature items are consolidated into nourishments.

Goals: I dumped the general store. Truly. I received the products of the soil markets and pastry kitchens as my own, rather than choosing the one-stop-shop.

I began eating bread the cook could discuss the formula of, generally just flour water and salt, and ate foods grown from the ground. I utilized vegetable oils and an entire store of coconut milk and tofu from my neighborhood devoted tofu creator.

Going out to Eat

Going out to eat can be extreme in certain spots, for example, Greece, where veganism isn't boundless. While there are some veggie lover eateries in Athens, it's significantly harder to discover vegetarian nourishment on the islands or in littler urban communities. Our ongoing outing to Ionian was a debacle with respect to vegetarian nourishment.

Goals: If you realize where you're going, call ahead. Offer to book the eatery for your companions, consider the café and dispel any confusion air. They need your custom; they ought to be glad to satisfy you.

Social Settings

Most veggie lovers likely concur that eating vegetarian isn't too troublesome until it is in a setting with non-vegetarians.

When in doubt, I make an effort not to raise the way that I'm veggie lover since I need to stay away from the cross-examination that generally pursues. It appears that individuals get so affronted by individuals declining to eat a similar nourishment that they start interrogating vegetarians concerning everything. At the point when veggie lovers answer those inquiries honestly, they're informed that they're by and large excessively long-winded. Individuals appear to feel that just by referencing that your veggie lover you are passing judgment on them for not being vegetarian themselves. Subsequently, they go on edge and start posing inquiries. They wouldn't ask another meat eater.

Different Vegans

Let's get straight to the point that being vegetarian isn't sufficient to cause two individuals to get along. Unfortunately, the vegetarian development is loaded with terrible individuals, including racists and misogynists. At that point you have the veggie lover police that judge all that you do. Making associations with different veggie lovers who really concur with you on different issues, too, can be a significant test all by itself. In light of this numerous veggie lovers really like to manage all the cumbersomeness of being the main vegetarian in a given circumstance.

Chatting with non-vegans about being vegan.

In spite of the reality, the expression "vegetarian" doesn't mean you're from an evil religion, or should I say "satanic faction," it appears you may wind up treated as though you were from one. There are a lot of meat-eaters who still think veggie lovers are lower in the natural pecking order than themselves. The platitude is that you're eating their nourishment, and it'll never get old. I was frequently addressed why I was doing it, so I essentially said it was a test. It's difficult to discuss the purposes behind veganism without seeming like an evangelist.

Goals: Be contemplated, be courteous, clarify your perspective, and don't call them killers. On the off chance that they don't acknowledge contrasts, move towards a subject that isn't nourishment.

CONCLUSION

A Plant-based meal is a very good substitute for the normal meals that we have. It has a number of advantages that have been discussed in this booklet, as well as its fair share of challenges and the best way that you can beat them to incorporate a happy and fulfilling eating style. With a plant-based meal plan, any individual is able to beat a number of chronic diseases that are brought forth with the type of eating lifestyle that we all hold. Life is intense, severe and unforgiving. This book has been tailor-made for beginners who would like to start on a plant-based meal plans as it emphasizes on the advantages and reasons as to why we should take plant-based meals and having listed the reasons as to why vegetables are better than meat. Vegetables are known to reduce the risks of some diseases, and hence even the medical technicians do encourage that even for non-vegetarians that they should add a little bit more vegetables in their diets more than the meat or animal products. This book has listed down the types of food to avoid once one has started off with a plant-based meal plan so as to make the most out of the plant products. For beginners, the book is well furnished with the knowledge of the basics of a plant-based meal plan and how to go about it and stick to it.

Understanding the benefits of a plant-based meal plan to our body is essential. This book is well equipped with the benefits that impact us positively in our bodies once we choose to start taking more of plant-based meals. Having listed a number of health benefits, it is a big challenge for one to stick to one meal plan and hence the challenges and temptations of seeing other people enjoy animal products and not getting tempted to have a taste of it. This is covered in this book as a cheat day; this is the only day that one is allowed to eat a non-plant meal just for a day. One would decide to eat meat and animal product that are not similar to the ones that are in the plant-based meal plan. A plant-based meal plan will assist in a number of things, including reducing weight as well as improving the general health of the skin. This book is equipped with a monthly meal plan that will assist a beginner to follow and introduce themselves into a plant-based meal plan as a lot of people find it as a challenge on how a what to prepare as meals once they switch to a plant meal based eating plan.

The focal point of this work is to encourage people to consume a lot of plant products by noting down the importance and challenges that people with this kind of diets go through and giving solutions on how to beat them and lead a healthy lifestyle that will encourage them to eat a lot of plant-based meals. The knowledge in this booklet will assist anyone to lead a healthy and disease-free life.